I0037472

"Whether you are a novice or a seasoned sales v in *5 Star Selling* will contribute to your success. Lee Daviss sales sys tem will help you from hello to goodbye, from preparing for sales calls to managing your sales territory. By implementing these ideas you'll definitely be at the top of the sales profession."

— *Tom Ziglar, President/CEO, Ziglar, Inc., and Proud Son of Zig Ziglar*

"Excellent job! I found the book to be a quick and easy read (and I am a big critic of books that don't get to the point quickly). Remembering my early days as a "rookie" salesman, a book like this would have been very helpful. Lee has captured the most practical elements of selling."

— *Jim Cederna, former Chairman and CEO of Calgon Carbon Corp*

"There are many books on how to sell. This one is very practical and based on extensive experience. Try it."

— *Nigel Bell, former Global V. President Lubricant & Fuel Additives Business, Shell International*

"This is a great book for new salespeople. I wish it would have been available to me 18 years ago when I started in the field, especially coming from such a technical background. It would have been much easier for me to pick up many more practical ideas more quickly. Even though the company where I began my sales career had a fantastic sales training program, the fundamental sales topics covered in this book would have been most welcome. I feel that I could have gotten up to speed much more quickly and started bringing value to my company faster."

— *Stephanie J. Brady, Global Sales Team Leader, Bostik, Inc.*

"I think this book is a very solid offering to the literature of selling."

— *Pete Masterson, Author of Book Design and Production, Past President, San Francisco Bay Area Publishers Association*

"Lee made sales calls on me and many others in my company. After reading this book, I can see that he practiced what he preached. We were able to develop a long term trusting relationship which greatly benefitted both of our companies."

— *Jay McQuillan, former Sales Manager, Chemcentral*

in2wit® LLC
Post Office Box 6458
Kingsport TN 37663 USA
info@in2wit.com

Copyright ©2014 by Lee Davis

Cover art ©2014 Mary S. de Wit

ISBN 13: 978-1-935095-50-7
ISBN 10: 1-935095-50-1
ISTC : A10-2014-00000001-1

Library of Congress Control Number:
2013948686

in2Wit and colophon are trademarks of in2Wit Publishing, LLC.

Printed in the United States of America
10 9 8 7 6 5 4 3 2 1

5 STAR SELLING

★★★★★
FROM BEGINNING TO
EXCELLENCE

LEE DAVIS

Opportunity Knocks:
Improve Your Chances For Success

When you become acquainted with the ideas and approaches presented in *5 Star Selling: From Beginning to Excellence*, you'll increase your own sales capabilities. In addition, if you are part of a team, you have the opportunity to strengthen your sales force. Begin by asking your salespeople this question: "Who taught you how to sell?" You'll discover a simple truth. Many have had only minimal, if any, formal sales training. Yet sales training, follow-up coaching, and help in maintaining motivation will boost all the measurements of success: achieve or surpass quota, close bigger deals, shorten the sales cycle, increase revenue and make more money.

★ **Would you like help with a cost-effective way to train new or inexperienced salespeople that will give them a solid basis in the fundamentals of selling and improve their ability to handle every aspect of the selling process?**

★ **Would you like to minimize the time needed to help your salespeople achieve a high level of success, motivating them to further accomplishment?**

★ **Can you picture the boost in performance achievable by a rejuvenated sales force?**

In addition to giving this book to your new salespeople, add to your company's opportunities by taking advantage of our customized programs which include speaking engagements, general or targeted training, coaching, workshops, or specific talks to groups or individuals. Contact Lee Davis by phone (423-292-5767) or through the website: www.5starselling.com.

The print version of *5 Star Selling: From Beginning to Excellence* is offered through Barnes and Noble, Amazon.com, and other retail bookstores. Kindle and EPub versions can be purchased through Amazon, iBooks, Nook, and Kobo through their digital bookstores. The audio book, read by the author, is available through Amazon, Audible.com and iTunes.

TABLE OF CONTENTS

INTRODUCTION:
What Will You Gain From This Book?

Would you like to begin your sales career with top-notch training targeted at getting you up to speed quickly, no matter what you are selling? Would you like a go-to manual that will rejuvenate your skills and offer a sales tune up? This is the sales-training-in-a-book you've been looking for!

Many good books are filled with sophisticated ideas that should be part of a salesperson's toolbox. Those books offer advanced techniques on how to ask specific need-benefit or problem-definition questions which help the prospects understand how to benefit from your products or services and solve their problems. Some books discuss specific topics in detail, such as how to close a sale, or how to handle objections.

However, during my career in sales and sales management, I found there was very little readily available practical information for the *beginning* salesperson. It was difficult to find information on how to use simple and basic techniques and concepts to get in position to develop a relationship where the customer looks for ways to do business with you. That's the kind of relationship that makes you the customer's first choice, and that ultimately achieves your goal: having the customer buy your products or services.

5 Star Selling: From Beginning to Excellence is that missing sales book. This book provides new salespeople with the nuts and bolts of how to succeed in sales and also contains many great tips for more experienced professionals. It presents the lessons that I have learned in sales, sales management, and marketing in a thirty-year career with a Fortune 500 company.

Using the principles taught in this book, you will learn how to prioritize your customers and prospects, and how to organize your territory so you can make calls on key people more often and more efficiently. You will learn how to make appointments, and how to deal with voicemail and email. You will learn how to prepare for a sales call, how to understand the ebb and flow of the call itself, and how to use this knowledge to your advantage. You will learn the importance of follow-up and how and when to do it. You will learn how to use entertainment effectively, and how to make management your ally and not an obstacle. You will learn how to overcome the fear that sometimes keeps salespeople from performing up to their full potential. Most importantly, you will learn how to develop the kinds of relationships that make people want to buy from you.

This book focuses on the timeless basic aspects of the selling process. The information presented here will serve you well, even when encountering the future changes that occur as the sales profession continues to transform in order to meet new challenges. Trendy buzzwords and the "latest, greatest ideas" for selling come down the pike all the time. Some will be useful, many will not. However, the basic concepts, tools, and necessary skills taught in this book will always be important to your selling efforts and will provide an excellent foundation for success.

Along with the basics, you will also benefit from a few advanced concepts to consider. Some sales positions require many of these ideas and tools. Other "one shot" sales opportunities require only a few of them. When selling real estate, appliances, or cars, for example, you need to establish your credibility and a relationship with your customer quickly. Even in those one-time situations, knowing and using many of the basic tools in this book will help you sell those buyers and also bring them back to you the next time they are in the market looking for the goods or services you offer. You will also benefit from learning to develop "word of mouth" recommendations which will bring those kinds of buyers to your place of business.

Other types of selling require more frequent calling and follow-up. Mastering the essentials presented here will help you to develop the right kinds of relationships for any situation. This is a good time to mention a few basic concepts to have under your belt before proceeding. I would call them the **Three Rules of Salesmanship.** This is a short overview so I will be expanding on these and adding other ideas in more detail throughout the book.

1. Speak briefly with your prospect about something in which they are interested.

This generally applies no matter what type of selling you are doing, or what product or service you are offering.

In a retail store this could simply be a greeting. If you observe a customer examining a product (a car, an appliance, an article of clothing), you can ask, "May I help you find something?" and you may receive a yes or no answer. But if you ask, "Would you like to know more about this particular model (or item)?" it may help you learn more about what the potential customer is looking for and why they are in your place of business. Or perhaps in industrial selling you might ask about what products or services they are currently using so you will have a good place to start.

2. Then provide the customer with enough facts and benefits until he or she is convinced they are justified in buying.

This, of course, is the key portion of the selling process. The salesperson must educate and inform the prospect and provide examples of how the product or service might benefit that customer. ("This car goes from zero to 60 in 3.4 seconds, so you'll impress the teenaged boys in the neighborhood and scare all your friends." Here, the fact is acceleration, and the benefit is to impress.) This process generally takes longer when selling industrial products and/or services that a customer is buying repeatedly or specialty products to replace current products they are buying, but is critical nonetheless.

During this part of the process, the salesperson should elicit comments from the prospect to determine what needs/desires the prospect wishes to fulfill. Then the facts and benefits can be tailored to the particular situation. There may be many other facts/benefits of the product, but it is a waste of time to focus on them if it is not in the prospect's interest (for example, if the prospect wants a car that is comfortable and safe to drive, the fact of its acceleration may not be a major point in its favor).

Finally, the salesperson should (if possible) express a "word picture" of the prospect using the product/service, enjoying the product/service, and benefiting from it. This is more important in "one shot" selling, since in most industrial applications the prospect or customer typically is using a product or service like yours already.

3.   *Ask for the order — or the next step in the process — and shut up.*
I've had prospects take five minutes to think over a proposal — and if I'd said anything to distract them or interrupt their thought processes, the sales interview might have been over… and a failure.

These are very basic selling tools that are typically part of the various contact points in the selling process. Regular/repeat customers may not need as much convincing at each contact when trying to keep and grow your business, but stressing the features and benefits that are important to them should continue be done on a regular basis. In fact, doing this in later contacts with the "one shot" customers and your regular repeat customers is an important part of what is called the "aftersell." This confirms the satisfaction they obtained by purchasing from you, and will encourage them to come back to you for future purchases.

One school of thought says a person has to be a "born salesperson" to make it in sales, that there are people with natural talent and that's the reason for their success. Another school says a person can be taught and mentored to be a successful salesperson. My experience says it is a little of both. That being the case, what is it that makes a successful salesperson?

Years ago, a major business publication issued an article that concluded that every successful salesperson possessed two traits, empathy and drive. Empathy is necessary in order to really want to know and understand the person you are trying to influence. That is a major factor in developing relationships. Personal drive is the key that keeps one coming back even after rejection, continuing to call on the prospective client or "prospect" and working to make the sale. One of the strongest attributes of personal drive is determination. Determination keeps a person going until success is achieved. Empathy, drive, dedication, persistence, and patience, along with some basic mechanics and a little fine tuning, are the attributes of a top-notch salesperson.

If you enjoy the selling process, genuinely like people and let it show, and feel good about your company and what you are selling, your enthusiasm alone will achieve good results. But, if you master the basics and learn the "extras" when needed, you will have an even more successful and rewarding sales career.

All of the stories presented in this book are true. I have given many examples of how to do the right things correctly. Occasionally I have added a few stories that illustrate the "pitfalls" inherent in taking a wrong approach. The names have been changed in all of these examples to protect the innocent … and the guilty.

You can be assured that by the time you finish this book and put these ideas into practice, you will be well on your way to being the best salesperson you can be.

★ ★ ★ ★ ★
POINTS

This book will give you:
- ★ Important basic tools to help you sell now, and in the future
- ★ Proven approaches to use in all types of selling
- ★ Information on prioritizing and organizing your territory
- ★ Proven skills for getting appointments with the right people
- ★ Sales call and follow up techniques
- ★ Tips for building customer relationships
- ★ Power to overcome fear and build confidence
- ★ Advanced concepts and ideas for achieving excellence

CHAPTER 1: MOTIVATION
What Charges Your Batteries?

What makes you want to be in sales? Is it just a job or do you really like it? Do you enjoy the "game" aspect of sales or is it just a series of activities to you? There are lots of reasons why people choose sales as a career. Some like the challenge of persuading others to their point of view and some like the satisfaction of being the person who influences decisions. Some thrive on the competition and some enjoy analyzing and solving problems that benefit them and others. Some get very interested in the possibility of making big money for doing something they enjoy. What excites you when getting out of bed every day? Are you self-motivated so that you don't need someone standing over you telling you what to do? Do you get charged-up by doing things yourself? Of course, many of the drivers that entice people into sales careers are important in other careers as well, but being in sales gives many people the opportunity to do activities they like in a job that really fits their personalities and interests.

Let me begin with a story. I was the sales manager in a new business venture where one of our technical service people, Paul, had expressed an interest in sales. A territory was open so we decided to give him an opportunity. He went through our solid sales training program and was sent to a previously untapped territory to sell our new product. After a year on the job, even with help, encouragement, and coaching, Paul had sold very little. I made the necessary, unpleasant trip to his region to explain that things had to start happening or he would be let go. During our discussion, he became very defensive and began relating many excellent excuses about why it was not his problem. I tactfully explained that where the problem lay didn't matter because, in sales, results were what counted. As expected, Paul went home that night quite upset with me and with the situation in general.

The next morning's meeting was very interesting. Paul and I met at my motel for breakfast, where he proceeded to tell me that he had just had his first good night's sleep in a long time. He told me he hated sales. He would sometimes get sick to his stomach before forcing himself to go out and make calls. He had a hard time getting appointments, and when people told him "no" he could not stand the rejection. The job was a nightmare for him, and he believed it might actually be contributing to a few health problems.

Paul said that our discussion the night before, although very unpleasant, had relieved the pressure. He had decided that — for him — selling (or sales) wasn't going to get any better, so he was ready to call it quits. If you are like Paul, in a job you hate, then get out of it. Life is too short to spend time working at something you don't want to do! A lot of sales books will tell you that "anyone can sell," but they often don't ask if everyone *should* sell.

Paul's situation is extreme, to be sure. Fortunately, we are all different and there are innumerable opportunities for different kinds of work. With some searching, almost anyone can find a rewarding and enjoyable career.

The postscript to Paul's story was that, luckily, we were able to find him another job in the company in technical service — his former career. If, unlike Paul, you like the sales process and lifestyle, just realize that sales is a "no excuses" career. Your success is up to you, and results, not activities, are what count. You don't have to possess an Ivy League education, or know the "right" people. You don't have to be an extrovert who has to be around people to recharge. Some of the best salespeople I know are introverts. It is, however, essential to like people and to be willing to develop good relationships.

Your motivation for selling is extremely important, so determine what keeps you going and hold on to it. If you've had a taste of sales and enjoy the people you meet, the ever-changing environment, the satisfaction of persuading people to go with you, and the rewards that come with tangible results, this book will help you be a better salesperson. It's a great career!

★★★★★
POINTS

★ Know yourself
★ Do you have the strong interests and personality attributes that are needed to be successful in sales?
★ Pick the career right for you
★ Determine your motivation for being in sales and hold on to it

CHAPTER 2: GETTING ORGANIZED
Maximize Your Effectiveness

This chapter is designed for those salespeople who have groups of customers and prospects that need to be called on regularly in order to develop or maintain business. If your customers come to you, as in real estate or automotive sales for example, this material may be less useful. In those situations, the salesperson will have to maximize methods such as advertising or "word of mouth" for getting customers in the door or on the phone. At that point, the rest of the material in this book will prove helpful, but organizing a sales plan is not usually a problem. Of course, organizing for follow-up or call-backs can still be extremely important and some of the same methods may be used.

Organizing a call plan is an important first step for sales territories that you need to cover on a regular basis. This particular topic is complex and, requires close attention because it builds the foundation for your selling process. I'm sure you've heard the expression, "Work smarter, not harder." That's what up-front organization is all about. It helps you be more efficient and allows you to spend your time in the right places, taking the most important steps toward achieving your goals.

Many companies have decided to streamline the kind of territory organization I will be describing here. Theirs will be much "looser" and considerably less structured. More leeway is given to the salesperson from the beginning to operate as he or she sees fit. Those companies often rely on the sales manager to watch and make sure everything is done correctly. This can be a problem if the sales manager is overworked or not close enough to the accounts or salespeople to supervise needed corrections. A more structured call plan system reduces the need for enhanced supervision and, when set up properly, makes it easier for the salespeople to do their jobs more effectively because they are free to focus more on selling. Based on my experience as a sales manager, working with several companies using many different plans, I am convinced that a more structured approach works much better, especially for new or inexperienced salespeople and those whose personalities need help in the organizational area. More structured call plans may be "relaxed" when the salesperson becomes more experienced and covering the accounts at the appropriate intervals becomes second nature.

Some salespeople's personalities are more oriented towards people, relationships, and the "big picture" rather than towards details. They may look at details as a distraction from selling, and sometimes get bogged down and overwhelmed. For them, this may be one of the more difficult parts of the selling process. It can be easy to get off the track. If you are this type of person, improving your organizational skills — not only in planning but in other day-to-day aspects of your sales job — is crucial to a successful sales career. Getting your territory organized means prioritizing your customers and your prospects, and then creating a schedule so that the proper amount of time and effort is allocated to each. Your company may have a specific format that they want you to use; if so, the following information may help you in working with that. If a format is not available, this chapter offers one to guide you in putting a call plan together.

The first step in your plan is to prioritize your current customers. If you take over a territory from an experienced salesperson the information needed to do that may already be available to you in background information from your predecessor. In growing companies where business is advancing such that new salespersons are added, and territories are rearranged as a result, you may get one "carved out" of several other territories and the information needed to prioritize accounts can still be obtained. If your territory is brand new with no prior calling by anyone at your company, you will need to do some research as you begin the selling process until you get enough information to do a proper analysis of the potential accounts. That may come from telephone calling, industrial guides, web sites, or from your initial calls on your prospects. Your sales management can also offer assistance in getting that information. Taking stock of these different situations plays a big part in knowing how to prioritize your initial plan which you can then revamp if needed as you gain experience.

In any of these cases, in order to prioritize your accounts you will need to know how much they buy, and you will also need to estimate how much selling effort will be needed to get — or keep — that business and make it grow. If you have a significant portion of their business and a good relationship, you will want to expend enough effort to keep it that way. Since it is usually easier to keep and grow business than to get new business, you cannot afford to take those customers for granted. If you lose current customers due to negligence or mistakes, they can be incredibly difficult to get back. It is better, in the beginning, to call on established customers more than you think is needed if you have time to do so.

In order to prioritize prospects you will need to know their buying potential in order to set up your calling frequency. As mentioned previously, you may need to make changes later, but that will come naturally after you are more familiar with your territory and the accounts. In some cases, you will find that following the call plan guidelines presented in this book will bring you business at new accounts relatively easily. That is because many salespeople are inept, and you will be welcomed by *their* customers because of *your* regular calling pattern and the sales skills you have obtained from this book. In other cases, you will find that getting business at a particular new account is so difficult that you are better off reducing the number of calls in your plan and spending your time and talents on more promising accounts. Generally, it's somewhere in between. As you become familiar with the accounts which have the potential to become good customers, you can better assess the effort and commitment required to get business and then make necessary adjustments as they become apparent over time. A discussion of possible changes to your plan with your sales management can often help you with these decisions.

Companies often use different criteria to measure an account's potential. Typically it is sales revenue, but sometimes it will be based on profitability if that differs substantially among the products and services being offered. A model can be built using profitability, but I have used sales revenue in the examples since that is more common.

Let's start by assuming you now have enough information using whatever metrics your company measures to begin your process of prioritization. At that point, how do you put together a call schedule or pattern? Territory size is a major factor. If your territory is small, it is relatively easy. With a small geographic territory it often pays to see customers who are in the same general neighborhood on the same trip. The efficiency that comes with making calls this way may enable you to work in an extra call or two a day, and that's a significant percentage of additional time in front of the customer. If you cover a large territory, perhaps several states, or even several countries, it is more difficult. You will have to plan your call frequency based on geographical proximity to be efficient and effective. That's easy to plan but sometimes difficult to implement.

As noted earlier, the first step is to group your customers and prospects based on their importance. Obviously, you can have as many groups as you like, depending on how often you need to call on the most important clients. Working for a large company, we found that we typically needed to call on customers on a schedule of every three, four, or five weeks, depending on their size and needs. For extremely large corporate accounts, our salespeople usually visited there every week.

There are two excellent ways to make sure you see customers and contacts as often as you should. These organizational plans will work well whether you are selling industrial products, pharmaceuticals, software services, copiers, or any other type of product or service where repeat calling is necessary to obtain and keep business. No matter how many calls you decide are needed, either method can work for you. The first method requires more work up front, but may be more helpful if your territory is large and if you have to make calls in several areas or sectors. The explanation of how to do this may need more study to become clear; therefore detailed examples are included in Appendix I. If you inherit a call plan from a previous salesperson, it is a good idea to re-evaluate that plan after you become familiar with the territory, particularly if you are replacing someone who wasn't doing very well.

Sector Call Plan Method

The sector call plan is developed by first grouping your accounts by geographic area. You can think of this as a "clover leaf" type of plan, where each clover leaf is an area to cover. You may have three, four, or even five or more distinct geographic areas you will need to include. The ranking of the accounts determines how often you call on them when you travel to each area. Some you will call on every time, some every other time, and some every third or fourth time through that particular area. You generally want to call equally on customers and prospects with the same potential. In one case you are trying to keep and grow your business; in the other case you are trying to develop business. A detailed example of this type of plan is presented in Appendix I.

When I first started in sales, I used this method very effectively. At that time in my career, I was covering several states and had divided my territory into four areas and a four-week call cycle. Each week I would make calls in a different geographic sector or area, and the fifth week I started over. It took a month to cover the whole territory. I visited important accounts every time that I went through a specific area. Other accounts I saw every other time or less (some as few as every fourth time through the specific area), depending on their importance. Working a plan like this means that any interim problems that might arise usually can be handled by telephone or email, and at the next scheduled visit you can take care of any follow-up details that need to be handled in person. If your territory is small geographically, you can just interrupt your schedule for a day and handle it personally, if you wish, and then go on with the plan where you left off.

One day, an important customer — with whom I visited every month when I was scheduled to work in his area — said to me, "It's amazing; I can look at my calendar and know when you are coming. It's like clockwork." Of course, I took vacations occasionally, and missed him when he was out once in a while, but in his mind, I was "Mr. Dependable." That's what you want your customers to think. Most salespeople are not that consistent.

You will notice with a plan like this that the medium-sized accounts can be called on less frequently — for example, every other cycle through a geographic area — and the small ones every fourth cycle through the area. They can be spread around in your plan so that, along with the important accounts you are seeing every time, you are seeing *different* less important accounts on each visit to the area. This allows you to allocate most of your time to the larger accounts but to still see the smaller ones as often as appropriate. Additionally, if you miss one of the medium-sized or small ones on a cycle through the area, you can catch up with them on the next trip to that area without getting very far out of the pattern.

I have worked this kind of plan with as few as three sectors and as many as six. The time it takes to cover one area or sector on each cycle can be a week or more or as little as a few days. If you cannot divide the geographic sectors so that you have about the same number of important and less important accounts in each, then vary the size of the sectors. One area/sector may take a week to cover while another one may only take three days. The key is that you will still see the larger accounts on every cycle through a geographic sector or area and the smaller ones on alternate cycles. You can coordinate areas that require two days to cover with those that require a week or longer, to see the accounts you need to visit in that area. This approach is flexible so you can decide what works best for you. The plan will work well even with your medium size and smaller customers. For those accounts that buy from you but are not large enough or do not have enough additional potential to warrant more time, this should be enough calling for you to keep their business. Because they are small, the competition cannot afford to call on them very often either. If you just see them regularly — even every other cycle for medium size customers, or every fourth cycle if they are small — the amount of attention you will give them will generally be more than they get from anyone else, and your current business will not be in jeopardy.

It is true that you may not have the opportunity to sell to many of the medium size or small prospects if they are getting good treatment from their current suppliers. That's because you will be calling on them less often than the larger ones, as these plans suggest. However, keep in mind that if you have prioritized correctly you will be putting most of your effort where you have the best opportunities to achieve maximum results. By still seeing these smaller accounts that are not buying but have some potential, even on a limited basis, you will be aware of any changes, such as a new competitive salesperson, dissatisfaction with their current supplier, or some other event which may open the door for you. If or when this occurs, you will be ready to upgrade the account and step in at whatever level of calling and service seems appropriate to develop business. You will also find that sometimes the salespeople from current suppliers will become complacent, and by staying in touch with those prospects — even every other time or so through the sector — you may find an opening where you can develop a profitable relationship.

This type of planning may seem complicated, and it takes some time to think through and set up, but it is a very effective process for investing the appropriate amount of time and effort on each account. Trying to set up appointments with people on a hit-or-miss basis is very difficult, inefficient, and generally much less effective. If you rely on your memory without a plan, you'll be saying things to yourself like, "When did I see ABC Manufacturing last?" or, "Who haven't I seen in a while?" or, "I want to go to that area to see XYZ, but I just saw DFG there last week and need to be somewhere else."

A sector call plan of this type will eliminate those thoughts and problems and make appropriate calling simple and consistent. In my experience, consistency is of critical importance to customers and will also be impressive to prospects you are trying to sell.

After you have developed the data and your plan you can make it much easier — and you can become more productive — by incorporating those details in a powerful software program like *Sage ACT!*, *Salesforce*, or others that are similar, that when set up properly will do most of the work for you. Software of this type, which often includes many other features, will keep track of your contacts and have details about them at your fingertips.

CUSTOMER CONTACT CALL PLAN METHOD

The second method of grouping is the customer contact call plan. This concept works best when you have a territory that is mostly in one geographic area, and when it is relatively easy to get to the different accounts with appropriate frequency but without giving up much efficiency. It is also useful when you have large or corporate accounts, which may not be geographically close, where there are many individuals you must contact at each company. You may need to see people in purchasing, technical (or research and development) departments, manufacturing, production, or any number of different functions, all of which may be critical to your success with the account. Usually, it is unlikely or even impossible to schedule appointments with them all in one visit.

With the customer contact call plan method, as with the sector call plan, it's still important to rank your customers in terms of time and effort needed. In most cases, the number of people you need to see at regular intervals for each account will be in proportion to the size of the potential account. With this method, you think about how often you need to see each contact, not just the individual companies.

In order to do this, put together a grid or spreadsheet with each company listed in the first column. Under each company (customer or prospect), list every important contact at that company. In the second column, next to the name of each contact at the various companies, put in the number of times per year you plan to see the contact. Then add columns for each week of the year, and note which weeks you want to schedule your calls. You will try to see some contacts weekly or monthly, others every other month (or even less). When you make the calls, put a notation of some type in the box under that week, so you can make sure you are visiting them the planned number of times per year. You will see the pattern develop as you make the calls according to your plan.

This kind of plan quickly answers the question, "Whom do I need to see next?" When you are setting up appointments, by looking at the plan you can easily determine where you should call and whom you should see. If something occurs that requires you to see someone "out of order," or a new contact must be added into the plan, you can accommodate the change while seeing other contacts at the same company. If entertainment is part of your effort, you can schedule it at appropriate levels and intervals. A clear example of how to set up this approach is given in Appendix I. Notably, much of this can be handled easily by devoted software applications (some of which are suggested in Appendix III).

I believe you will find that one of these two methods, or some combination of the two, will serve you well. Nothing about them should be rigid; it's your plan. As you develop more knowledge about the customers and prospects, adjust the details as often as needed. Sometimes your most important customers will not want see to see you as often as you like, and occasionally your smaller customers will try to demand too much of your attention. Having a plan will help you balance and work out that potential problem. As mentioned, if more explanation is desired, step-by-step instructions and examples of how to set up these plans are included in Appendix I.

As I noted previously, many companies do not expect their salespeople to use more structured kinds of call plans, but in my experience they are extremely valuable, especially if you are a new salesperson. Once these kinds of call plans are put together, you can concentrate on selling, and not worry about where you need to be. It's much easier to "Plan your work, and work your plan."

Remember, putting together an organized call plan will save you time in the long run and ensure that you are seeing the most important people as often as you should and when you should. It will maximize the time you spend at the most important customers and prospects, and also make sure you do not neglect smaller "bread and butter" accounts. It also gives you the flexibility to occasionally allow deviation from your call plan to "put out fires," and then be able to easily go back to it without losing sight of the big picture. Knowing you are "covering your territory" by following an appropriate, well thought out plan will make the most effective use of your time, boost your confidence, and bring desirable results.

★★★★★
POINTS

- ★ Prioritize your accounts
- ★ Evaluate the geographic area you will be covering
- ★ Assemble a call plan
- ★ Use appropriate software or spreadsheets to make keeping track of everything much easier
- ★ Plan your work, and work your plan
- ★ Keep the big picture in mind, even when "putting out fires"

CHAPTER 3: STARTING STRONG
What Do You Have to Know About
Your Company and Its Products to Begin?

The short answer to what you need to know about your company and its product is: *as much as you can.* That may be relatively easy if your product line is narrow or your services are limited. It can be very difficult if you have a broad or technical product line, or are offering many services.

Let's start with your company. Where does it fit in the markets it serves? Is it a large market leader that does significant research and development and is constantly bringing out new products or services? Perhaps your company is at the other end of the spectrum and primarily tries to copy the leaders. Your company may be producing the products at least as efficiently, and can be more aggressive in marketing them because you do not have the higher costs associated with research and development. Perhaps, as is more typical, your company is a mixture of both. Where your company fits will differ, based on the specific products or services offered. The point to all of this is that you need to know where you fit, so that when you are talking to a customer you can sell your company and the way it does business. Companies can be very different in the way they approach various markets, yet each can have a distinct advantage that can be used effectively.

If, for example, your company operates as one of the market leaders in areas of your customer's interests, you can make the case that they need to be seeing you and buying from you so that they will be on the cutting edge of future developments. You will probably have access to more market information and can make some of that available to the customer as appropriate. You have the opportunity to bring a lot of extra value to that customer or prospect. Naturally, you don't want to give that away.

If your company doesn't happen to be one of the market leaders, you may still have some strong selling points. Perhaps you are able to offer more advantageous pricing because your company may have lower costs than the market leaders. Or you might be more nimble in moving to new things and following new market trends, because it is sometimes difficult for market leaders to change directions in a hurry. This is often the case when the latest new thing wasn't their idea or invention (the NIH or "not invented here syndrome"). The key is that almost all companies have some advantages or they wouldn't be in business. Know what those are for your company and learn how to sell them effectively.

Now consider your products or services. Are they unique, specialty items or commodities? Do you supply most of the market needs, or are there many others competing with what are essentially the same products? You need to know exactly where your products or services fit into the market, because that will determine, in many cases, how you should be selling them. Unique or specialty products or services are usually sold on specific attributes or properties that demonstrate their superiority to others offered for the same purpose. Those kinds of benefits generally allow higher prices in the process. If you are selling specialties, you will need to be very familiar with what makes them better and how to present that to customers. If you have not clearly differentiated those products, the customers will often try to turn your specialties into commodities. They can then push for a lower price, inferring they can get the same product or service elsewhere. That's why knowing the specific features of your specialty products or services, and selling the differences that these features offer, is very important. If you are new to your company, you can determine that information by talking with your company's technical people and learning from them the special attributes of these products and services. Study the product brochures or technical data sheets, noting particularly the areas where what you are offering is different from any competitive materials, until you have those differences firmly fixed in your mind. And pay close attention to the customers already buying those specialties and the reasons why they are buying.

Also, ask your sales manager and others in your company to help you identify competitors in each of your product lines and to give you information about what to expect from them. If you can get access to them, review the brochures and technical data sheets of those competitors as well. It's a good idea to talk with other salespeople at your company who are having success selling your products or services, and to find out what they feel is important about them and what approach works best for them. Suggest that your management include "success stories" as part of the sales meetings, so you can continually learn how others are being successful.

If you are selling commodity items, which are typically the same as or very similar to products widely available from several sources, it often comes down to price plus the perception of you and your company in the eyes of the customer. Even in these situations, you still need to know as much as you can about your product and where it and your company fit in the commodity market. You will also need to learn your company's approach to selling products in commodity markets. Sometimes products may seem the same on the surface, but there are often subtle differences that you can emphasize. As we already noted, don't forget that a great source of information about your products and services are your current customers. They are buying for many different reasons, and those reasons should be well known within your company as valuable resources you can use when selling to others. Knowing all the material discussed here is very important because if you are not sold on your company and its products and services, no one else will be either. These concepts are still very important in one-shot or short cycle selling. For example, selling a Cadillac is different from selling a Chevrolet. The former is a high-end luxury vehicle while the latter usually is not. Selling a sedan is different from selling an SUV or minivan. Brands convey divergent messages to different people in terms of quality and company reputation. You will need to learn the attributes of your brands, and how and why they appeal to specific people, or groups of people, and sell accordingly.

If you are doing a good job of selling what your company has to offer, and you are competitive price-wise, you — as the salesperson — can make the difference. And, interestingly enough, even if it looks like everything is not going your way, you can sometimes come out on top. As a sales manager, I worked with a salesperson who was in this situation. Together, we called on a purchasing agent representing a significant account. During the call the customer turned to me and said, "You know, sometimes I am amazed. I often don't like what your company does very much. You are always trying to sell me at the highest prices and occasionally have even sold me inferior product. You jerk me around when the market is tight and then expect me to buy when things loosen up. Even with all those problems, you have most of my business. Do you want to know the reason why?"

She stopped and pointed to our salesperson and said, "Because of him; I know and like him, I trust him, and he is always making sure that I am treated right in the end, no matter what happens along the way. I can count on that. And that's why I buy from him. I just wanted you to know how valuable this guy is to you."

This can be *you*, a salesperson who understands how to sell what you have in that situation… you! Know your products intimately. Know what your company has to offer. But also never forget that the customer buys your company's products not from a faceless supplier, but from you. So sell yourself. Many of the following chapters will help you learn how to do just that.

★ ★ ★ ★ ★
POINTS

★ Know where your company fits into the market:
   What keeps it in business?
★ Know your products or services:
   What are their unique attributes?
★ If you're not "sold," no one else will be either
★ Know why your current customers buy from you
★ Know your competition and its products or
   services
★ Remember, customers buy from people, so sell
   "*you*" as well

CHAPTER 4: FEAR
"We Have Met the Enemy and He Is Us" —Pogo

Fear is the enemy of the salesperson. As I mentioned in Chapter 1, where we covered motivation, it sometimes becomes such a huge problem that it can ruin a salesperson's career. Fear is what you feel when you are getting ready to make appointments and you think you may not be able to get them. Fear is what you feel when you must go in and face a customer who has a problem. Fear is what you feel tugging at your insides when you ask a customer to do something, facing the possibility they might say "no." Fear is what makes you procrastinate when faced with any disagreeable task. Fear is why you wait until tomorrow to call the customer about a problem, even though you know that problems inevitably get worse with inattention. I have seen fear paralyze salespeople to the point that they were totally ineffective.

All salespeople feel fear to some degree at one time or another. They may not want to admit it, or call it fear, but that's what it is. The key is not whether — or how — you feel it, but how you handle it. Successful salespeople take their fears and use them to create positive situations. For them, fear is a catalyst to greater achievement. Conquering those uneasy feelings, and going ahead in spite of them, releases incredible energy and vitality. It's like a weight is lifted and you are free to burst forth with new purpose.

When you find yourself with all sorts of "good reasons" for putting off or not doing disagreeable tasks, taking a closer look may reveal these are excuses, simply a disguised form of fear. I'm sure you have heard the expression "fake it until you make it." The discipline to do this is what's required to overcome reluctance or even paralysis.

Personal discipline in selling is extremely important. If you can face those fears and force yourself to persevere, they will eventually disappear. That's because when you achieve excellence, you have nothing more to fear. When you become good at making appointments, asking questions, answering objections, solving problems, or whatever else you feel uncomfortable doing, the fear of facing those things goes away. You know you can handle those challenges with no problems. Experience and increasing competence put you, not fear, in charge. Making appointments with potential *new* clients or customers was a difficult problem for me in the beginning. I was always trying to put it off by thinking of other "more important" things I had to do instead. However, if you never see new potential customers or clients your current business will eventually fade away due to normal attrition. Knowing that, I just had to make myself pick up the phone and start calling, even though it was very uncomfortable at first. But as I developed things to say that would interest the prospects, and called more and more people, it became much easier. It never became high on my list of favorite things to do but, as I practiced and became competent at making these kinds of appointment calls, they no longer caused apprehension. I don't know which parts of the selling process may be difficult for you, but I can promise you that if you discipline yourself to do them over and over, and practice, you will get better and it will get much easier.

With most things, when you *practice* you improve. In sales, the key word is to practice those basic skills until you achieve excellence. Practice on smaller accounts where the stakes are smaller until you become proficient. If you are put into a difficult situation at a large account and make a mistake, admit it to the customer and learn from it. People respect you when you admit errors and, usually, just by doing that your fear goes away. After all, if everyone knows you goofed, why worry about it anymore? Just let your client know that you will do better the next time. If you admit an error to a customer, he will know that you are the kind of person who tells him about problems and he will trust you more. *Customers hate surprises more than mistakes.*

You have to be willing to laugh at yourself occasionally. This doesn't mean that you should not take the customer or prospect's concerns seriously, but don't always take *yourself* so seriously. I know selling is your livelihood and career, but it may help to think of sales as a game. *No one* wins every time. The fun is in the doing, the challenges, and the successes — and not in the failures. In sales, failures and rejections of some type are commonplace, so don't let the fear of them be a factor. Remember, if you do not fail occasionally, you are not out of your "comfort zone." If you stay in your comfort zone and there is no potential for failure, you will never reach the success you are capable of achieving. You will only expand your comfort zone, and your ability to achieve more, if you constantly attempt to exceed your own perceived limitations.

Continue to persevere, to practice, and to make any fears that you have spur you on to be more creative and energetic in pursuit of your goals. The successes you have will be the "highs" that makes sales such an enjoyable career.

★ ★ ★ ★ ★
POINTS

- ★ Every salesperson feels fear at times
- ★ Don't let fear paralyze you
- ★ Fake it till you make it ... *practice*
- ★ As you become more accomplished, fear disappears
- ★ Continually strive to expand your "comfort zone"
- ★ Success breeds energy, creativity, and more success

CHAPTER 5: MAKING APPOINTMENTS
How Do You See the Important Contacts?

In my job as a sales manager, I found that making appointments was one of the most difficult things for a new salesperson to learn how to do well. Many new salespeople become discouraged when they encounter resistance and have difficulty with their first attempts. The fear of rejection can rear its ugly head. The mechanics of making appointments are pretty simple, but can be tough to put into effective practice. Here are a few techniques that have worked well for me.

Since voice mail is so predominant, making appointments is getting more and more difficult. Very few people answer their own telephone, making planning ahead even more important. This is especially true in trying to get first-time appointments with prospects who do not know you at all. I've seldom heard a voice mail that didn't say something like, "Leave your number and a brief message and I'll call you back."

Sadly, most of the time you never get that call back, especially in the beginning when they don't know anything about you. Usually, until I got to know the person I was trying to reach, I would not leave voice mails expecting them to call back. I would just allow enough time to make several attempts until the customer *could* be reached on the phone in person. I would make notes in my calendar to ensure I did not forget about making regular call-backs until I was finally able to reach the individual I wanted to meet. Usually, when you are persistent, you will eventually get a chance to talk with someone in person to discuss arranging that first appointment. If, after several attempts, you find they never answer their phone personally, you may finally have to leave voice mails in an attempt to get an answer. If they don't respond to voice mails (and some never do), you might have to move to a more drastic approach. With hard-to-contact prospects, I occasionally had to finally resort to leaving a message like this: "I've been unable to reach you and I know you are busy. However, I wanted to discuss an idea (or whatever you think is right to insert here) that may be important to you so I'll be in your area next Wednesday and would like to stop by around 3:00 p.m. for a few minutes. Please let me know if that time is not good for you and we can try for another possibility. My number (or email) is ..."

Sometimes you will find that the person didn't call you back to let you know he or she would be busy and, when you arrive, still can't see you. At that point, if you are courteous, you have usually generated enough guilt on their part that you will be able to arrange a later appointment on the spot or have a chance to see them the next time. If you are going to try this technique, it should be a last resort. You can run the risk of alienating the potential customer before getting started. However, when it comes down to the point where you have nothing to lose, why not give it a try?

Another method available today that sometimes works well in getting initial appointments is email. If you can obtain the email address of the person you want to meet, you can prepare a message that will "leave them hanging," wanting to hear what you have to say. You can then try for the appointment in the email, giving them some choices, or you can let them know you will be calling to set something up. You may want to check out current online services that provide an appointment interface between you and your client with possible openings. You can't do that before a relationship is established, but you may earn approval for this later. Some people may find this an immediate and simple way to choose a good time for an appointment and to respond to you. You should be sensitive to the fact that some people may find this impersonal. If so, note in your client file that this prospect prefers to receive phone calls for arranging meetings. Occasionally you will need to try to arrange an appointment with someone acting as a *gatekeeper*: a receptionist, secretary, executive assistant or someone in another type of intermediate position between you and the person you are trying to see. Gatekeepers typically will be reluctant to give you the email address of the person you want to contact, but they will often give you their own email address so you can send them information that they can forward. This gives you an opportunity to insert benefits, hooks, or teasers in your email and, hopefully, you will intrigue the principle person enough so that someone will get back to you or you can follow up to plan an appointment.

Assuming a prospect or client *does* answer their phone, it's good to be respectful of their time. I usually identify myself, ask how they are doing and if they have a minute or if it's a bad time to call. If they say they are in the middle of something, I ask when they might be free so I can call back. Sometimes rather than have you call back, they want a "quickie version" right at that moment about why you called, so you better be ready with a short presentation that will "hook" their initial interest. Occasionally, they will just give you another time when they can talk, and you can arrange to make sure you call back at that time. Of course, if you take the approach of asking if they are free, and you agree to call back, you always run the risk of getting back to a situation where it takes a long time for them to finally answer the phone in person again.

When you finally get in touch with your prospect it is always important to be prepared with some kind of "teaser" to talk about that will create some interest. Something effective might be a "new product or service" your company offers that is better than what's currently available for some reason. Telling them that you will be bringing a short demonstration or appropriate visuals is typically good. Samples of successes are one of the best ways to develop the interest of the prospect. Your products or services must have some attractive features or your company wouldn't be in business. Learn to create "catch lines" or phrases that will pique the customer's interest.

When our company was introducing a new line of water-based inks, I used to say that our new products were water-based inks that performed like solvent based inks (products currently used in the industry) and I wanted to show them some printed samples. Since the industry was trying to move away from solvent-based inks for environmental reasons, I could usually get the first appointment. The second and third appointments depended on their application and the perceived value of my product. Remember, in most cases you are not trying to make a sale on the first visit. You are trying to generate enough interest so that the customer will want to hear or learn more and will be amenable to future appointments. Sometimes you can do that by selling your company. If you sell for a major supplier of goods and services in your field, point out that even though the customer is not buying from you, he or she might want to stay in touch with all the players for better information about what's going on in the market. Then make sure you have something valuable to bring to the visit in terms of information. Sometimes they will send you on to see R & D, laboratory people, engineers, or others inside their company, but at least your foot is in the door with some of the decision-makers.

When making appointments, it is always important to offer choices. If I was going to be in the area for several days, after my "developing interest" statement, I would say something like, "I'll be in your area next Wednesday and Thursday. Which day would be better for you?" If they are busy those days, you might say something like, "Well, I really wanted to see you while I was there, so I'll make some adjustments in my schedule. Would Monday or Friday perhaps be better?" Then you can nail down morning or afternoon, etc. If you are only going to be in the area for the day, then you use the same technique but offer a choice of morning or afternoon. If your sales budget can afford lunches, inviting them to lunch will sometimes do the trick for people who always seem to be busy. After all, they have to eat sometime. Lunches can be tough to set up for the initial call, because they don't know you at that point and may not be quite ready to commit to spending that much time with you. You might try to open the door by suggesting an alternative way to meet: "I know you are extremely busy so perhaps lunch may be the only opportunity we have to fit in a short discussion; could we do that?" Or, if they won't "do lunch" but they give you an appointment which results in a pleasant first call experience then the ice is broken and lunches are usually easier to put together in the future. I wouldn't hesitate to suggest it for my first visit if it looked like the only way to see the person. Again, at that point, what do you have to lose?

Flexibility and polite persistence with a good opening will usually work out eventually. There will be some people you'll never be able to see, no matter how hard you try. Don't let it bother you. It's their problem, not yours. I always told myself they just didn't know what they were missing, and usually that was the case. Companies who are not open to new things or the choice of other alternatives can eventually fall behind their competitors. Hopefully, with your products or services, their competitors will be your customers. Remember, your time is valuable. Make it count!

As you can see, the key to the first appointment is persistence and some sort of "hook" that will entice them to see you. The key to future appointments is in providing a pleasant experience for potential customers — and bringing enough value — so that they will be interested in hearing more. You will also find that the more you do it, the easier it gets. Practice on the less important potential customers first. Learn from your mistakes. You will get better.

To make regular follow-up appointments, you will need to find out what timing works best for your area. You will have to determine how far in advance you need to call to schedule appointments effectively. When I was making calls in the smaller Midwestern towns and cities, my accounts were pretty well scattered and they didn't see many salespeople. Since that was the case, I could typically make appointments just a day or two ahead and it was easy to get an appointment. When I was calling in Chicago, or in the highly populated Northeast, I had to make appointments at least a week ahead, and they were tougher to get. Sometimes you just have to experiment to see what works best.

After my call schedule was reasonably well established, and most of my customers and prospects knew me pretty well, I made a habit of trying to set up lunch appointments first with my most important accounts, and filled in around them. After all, how do you like talking about your products or services in the customer's office with the phone ringing and people sticking their heads in and out all the time? Isn't it better to be sitting together at a table in a restaurant for an hour or so with no distractions except deciding what to order for lunch?

Keeping track of your appointments in one place is crucial. You can use a daily planner, or one of the various electronic devices with a software program like *Windows Mail* or *Sage ACT!* installed. Since changes sometimes are needed you will want to keep your calendar readily accessible to make the necessary adjustments to your schedule. Find out what works for you and do it consistently.

Remember, when it comes to making appointments, especially in the beginning, be polite, be persistent, and be ready with something to get their attention. If you can do that, making appointments will not be a problem and you will be free to concentrate on other things.

★★★★★
POINTS

- ★ Making appointments is critical to your success
- ★ Learn how to make voicemail and email work for you
- ★ Know what makes your company and products unique
- ★ Be ready with short "interest developing" statements
- ★ Offer choices
- ★ Be polite but persistent
- ★ Consistently keep your appointments handy on whatever device you use so they can be rearranged if needed

CHAPTER 6: CALL PREPARATION
Be a Professional

Being unprepared for a call, whether in person or via some other method, is worse than unwise — it is inexcusable in the eyes of your prospects, and therefore counterproductive to your ultimate goals as a professional salesperson.

For cold calls (visiting companies you've never called on, but that appear promising) or leads you have been given to check out, be sure to learn something about the company before going in. Many of them will have websites that can be found by typing the company name into an internet search engine. This will usually give you plenty of information on the company, its products or services, and the markets they serve. For large companies, you might check online sites like Yahoo Financial, the Wall Street Journal, or other business publications devoted to your markets to see if there is any recent news. Imagine the irritation of a purchasing agent having his time wasted in hearing questions that could have been answered by the salesperson spending five minutes at the computer preparing for the call. If that's your first call on that prospect, it might well be your last.

An acquaintance of mine made a mistake early in his career that illustrates my point about preparation and professionalism. He was selling for a large manufacturer and heard that a company he had never called on used drum-sized quantities of one of his products in a hair-spray application. Typically, this material, when purchased in smaller quantities (for example, 50-gallon drums or 5-gallon pails), was usually handled by local distributors and not manufacturers, but he decided to pay the company a visit anyway. The plant was in a big city's industrial warehouse area not designed to welcome visitors. When he rang the bell, an individual came out to see him and took him to a small office. After introducing himself, my friend made the casual comment that he was out prospecting that day looking for "oddball" applications for his products. The prospect, who turned out to be the owner of the company, looked back at him and said, "Oddball applications? You think my business is an oddball application? You can leave right now and never come back!"

After that comment, the company owner proceeded to start going through paperwork on his desk as if no one were there, and the salesperson, after being ignored, finally left. Because of this cavalier approach, he insulted a prospect and obtained no information about requirements, prices, suppliers, or anything else. As it turned out, this prospect was a huge producer of hairspray and purchased his product in tank truck quantities from manufacturers like my friend's company. The salesperson told me later he had just gotten lazy and was ashamed of himself for being so unprepared and unprofessional. It was a major missed opportunity. It is wise to treat every prospect as a large potential customer and prepare accordingly until you learn otherwise.

There are several types of lead management software like *Leads 360*, *Dashboards*, *Leadmesh*, and others that will take you through the entire sales process with potential new customers. There is also software that will help you develop marketing campaigns that will capture the attention of new and current customers. Most of the time your company will be the one utilizing these approaches, but occasionally you may want to do an email campaign of your own to develop new leads or to get new information out to your customers.

If you are new to an area, you may want to get involved with the local trade organizations for the industries you are servicing. Important companies in the field are usually represented, so by joining these organizations, or at least getting a roster of the members, you can sometimes find new opportunities.

Many industries have at least two organizations. One is usually populated by people in purchasing, and you will find many of your competitor's salespeople in attendance at these meetings. That is often a good time to find out useful information about the "opposition" and how they operate. Many times these organizations are vehicles for entertainment opportunities like golf outings, holiday dinners, and other more socially-oriented occasions which can also offer valuable interaction. Typically, there are also trade organizations that are geared toward the technical people in that industry, and due to the nature of the discussions or presentations, there are often fewer salespeople at these meetings. Being involved with these types of associations will help you meet people who approve your products, or are responsible for developing new products. Obviously, this group can be very important to you — and usually there is less competition for their attention. Try out the various industry organizations until you determine which ones give you value for the time you will need to commit.

As you learn more about each company's potential, and about what effort will be required on your part, you can adjust the time spent preparing for the calls. In the beginning, as you are learning about the account, call preparation will take a little longer until you find out what is necessary and appropriate for each account.

Using the computer and other sources to check for new information about customers and prospects you already visit on a regular basis is also a good idea. As you will see later, information like this helps you bring value to the call, and the customers and prospects know you are doing your homework before seeing them. It's very important to review the latest sales data and read the last call report to make sure nothing you promised has been neglected. Be sure to make some brief notes in your daily planner or electronic device of what you plan to cover in the call. I will show you a good way to use those notes later.

It can be useful to prepare a "profile sheet" for each account. It should have the company's address and phone number and a brief description of how to find it. The contacts with titles and telephone numbers or company extensions should also be included. A sample profile follows:

ABC MANUFACTURING

1266 Old Stage Road
Blissville, Ohio, 36418
555-321-9000
FAX 555–321-9980

Contacts: (with email addresses)

Joseph Anderson – Purchasing Agent 555-321-9555
   janderson@abcmanufacturing.com
Doris Hill – Vice President 555-321-6759
   dhill@abcmanufacturing.com
Bob Parker – President
   bparker@abcmanufacturing.com
June Ball – Lab Manager 555-321-6645
   jball@abcmanufacturing.com
Dave Mist – Projects Engineer 555-321-6688
   dmist@abcmanufacturing.com

ABC manufactures remote switching apparatuses and
   offers software for their use.
Products used: chemicals, cleaning solutions, metals,
   etc.
Directions to the plant:
Route 321 from Lima, OH, into Blisssville. Right on
   4th street (after 1st National bank). After crossing
   the RR track, it is 2.3 miles on the left

You can, of course, make this profile sheet as brief or as detailed as you feel is necessary. You can add their "hot buttons." Do they like to go to lunch or dinner? Do they like morning or afternoon appointments? What are their interests? What do they look to you for? Maybe even specific information as to how they fit into the market. Again, as brief or detailed as you want. Keep this information on your electronic device where it is instantly retrievable. You may want to carry a print copy as a backup. As you can see, the information is changed infrequently, usually only for personnel changes, so it is relatively easy and, once prepared, takes very little time to keep it up to date. Glancing at it before each call will help you familiarize yourself with the information until it becomes second nature. If, for some reason, your company decides to make changes and someone else inherits the account from you, they will be very grateful for this information.

You are now prepared. In the next chapter, let's see how you conduct the actual call.

★★★★★
POINTS

★ Learn all you can initially about prospects
★ Stay up to date on current accounts
★ Always review the latest sales information
★ Use technological tools to keep information at your fingertips
★ Approach all calls in a serious professional manner
★ Join the appropriate trade organizations
★ Prepare useful, instantly available company profiles

CHAPTER 7: THE SALES CALL
Where the Rubber Meets the Road

The sales call is like the critical play of a big game. It's what you've prepared and practiced for so you can get that big win. What came before is important, and what comes after is also important, but this is you, on the stage, making it happen. What actions you take, and how you handle yourself during the sales call — face-to-face with the customer or prospect — are major factors in your success. Although this chapter is primarily oriented toward calling in person, many sales calls today are done on the telephone or through some sort of on-line interface. Some of the ideas presented here will be appropriate for these kinds of calls as well. Here are several tips on the mechanics of the call itself.

Constantly expand your knowledge about each account you are seeing.
What are you trying to find out? You need to learn what drives their business and what you can do to address those positively. You'll want to know as much as you can about their industry and where they fit in. It's important to know their competitors since they may also be potential customers for your products or services. It's also good to be aware of their current suppliers so you can analyze possible opportunities. Selling is all about the questions. This is especially important when you are first taking over an account or are brand new. The first few calls are critical for learning. During those initial calls you can ask questions that you would be embarrassed to ask on later visits. Open-ended questions work best here. Be sensitive to how you phrase inquiries, because you want the call to be a conversation, not an interrogation. After several calls, you will be expected to know most of the basic information about the account by both the customer and your management. Get it early so you won't appear ignorant later. Try to

learn something new each call, until you have a fully developed picture of what is going on. Take good notes so you can retain the new information you learn. It may be useful to add this additional information to your "profile sheet" on the customer so you will have it at your fingertips later, if needed.

Position yourself, your company, and your products or services correctly in front of the customer.

Where the customer or client sees you in the grand scheme of things may affect how they respond to your selling efforts. This is why you spent the time learning as much as you could about your own company, its products, its place in the market, and where your competitors fit. All of this information (see Chapter 3) gives you the necessary advantages to position yourself and your company in a more favorable position.

Make every effort to be punctual.

If possible, try to arrive a few minutes ahead of time. This will give you the opportunity to think about what you plan to accomplish on the visit and to review your approach to the call one more time. Most customers will give you a break if you are occasionally caught in traffic and are a little late. As a rule of thumb, if I was going to be more than about 15 minutes late, I would call and let them know why I was going to be late and what time I expected to arrive.

Treat everyone in your customer's organization with respect, from the receptionist to the president.

Every company has "formal" and "informal" networks of power. You want to recognize and try to become "plugged in" to both. If possible, cultivate the receptionist. Be friendly. If you are early for the appointment, and conversation seems to be welcome, chit-chat a little. Sometimes you can learn a lot about the company from a source like this. You may even learn about other important contacts you should be seeing at the company. In small companies, the receptionists often wear many hats and can have several other responsibilities. They may be the gate-keepers for purchasing, or an assistant or buyer who actually does the ordering. It's important to be liked and respected by these multi-functional individuals since they may influence buying decisions. That said, be respectful of *everyone* you come across, not for what they have to offer you, but because you know everyone is important. People learn what you are like by watching how you treat those who cannot necessarily help you. Realize that they have their own skills and talents and can do some things better than you can. Respect them for it.

You should be very conscious of making a good first impression.

Although most business dress is much more relaxed these days, it's still important to help create the right atmosphere. When I was calling on management at large customers in the big cities, I wore a suit and tie. When calling on folks at small companies in the rural Midwest I left the coat, and sometimes the tie, in the car. In most cases, I tried to dress slightly better than the person I was calling on. This was not a matter of one-upmanship or of trying to appear "elite;" it was just to encourage respect. Blend your role as a salesperson into the cultural context of your company and also of the people you will be seeing.

When I became the sales manager of a division of a large company, one of our salespeople was making calls in casual jeans and designer shirts, with a big gold medallion on a chain hanging around his neck. We had a discussion about the impression he was making. While he was welcome to express his tastes in his personal life, he needed to realize that while he was on sales calls he represented our company, and his dress conveyed a lack of respect toward our customers.

Your company may have some sort of dress code for salespeople. The classic case several years ago was IBM, when all the salespeople wore blue suits and white dress shirts. Even "Big Blue" has relaxed a little now. My original company used to require suits and ties; sport coats were not acceptable. After management began making calls in sport coats, things changed. If your company has a dress code, follow it. But, in doing so, keep in mind that you are ultimately responsible for the results, and it's the *customer* that has to feel comfortable.

Before entering your appointment, turn off your cell phone.

When you are talking with a customer, he or she is the most important person and should have your full attention. Answering a phone call while meeting with a client is disrespectful, rude and distracting.

Remember to respect your customer's time.

Everyone is different. Some people are "get to the point, very businesslike" types, and others are more "laid back and relaxed." Try to respond to each in the way that person would like. This is a very important concept. Sometimes you need to get in and get out relatively quickly, especially today when people are often doing more than one job and are extremely busy. Other times you have to just go with the flow. Try to develop that "sixth sense" that will tell you how things are progressing and when you have overstayed your welcome. When I began to cover my first sales territory, I made several calls with the salesperson I was replacing in order to get acquainted with the customers. I didn't know much about selling, but I did have a sense of timing. About the time I felt every call should have been concluded, we stayed an extra 15 to 30 minutes. It was obvious to me, but the person I was replacing didn't pick up on the customer's verbal and body language cues. When I was a sales manager later in my career, I noticed some salespeople really have a problem with knowing when to wind things up. Educate your senses and learn to listen to them. If you think you have a problem in this area, check yourself by asking people you travel with to give you their opinion when you review the call with them.

Here's a simple technique that worked well for me. Before going in to see contacts I called on regularly, I would make an abbreviated list of the points I was going to cover in my daily planner or electronic tablet. During the call, I would leave it open on my lap or on the edge of the desk so the person I was calling on could see it. They usually couldn't read what I had on it, but they could see I had an agenda.

The list might look like this:

* **Review sales**
* **Discuss late shipment**
* **Determine plant shutdown period**
* **Rust Manufacturing (their competitor) going out of business?**
* **Next quarter's projection**
* **New problems or opportunities**

After some appropriate small talk, I would say something like, "I have several things I would like to cover today but, before doing that, is there anything from your perspective that we need to discuss first?"

That gave the customers or prospects the opportunity to bring up things they felt were important and get them taken care of immediately. By addressing their concerns first, they weren't distracted thinking about them while I was covering the points *I* wanted to make. Many times, some of the things they wanted to discuss were on my list already. After we had finished with their items, I would then refer to my list and work through it. They could see me checking them off as we went along. They saw I was prepared and not wasting their time, and that each call had a natural endpoint. Another benefit of this technique is that you do not have to worry about whether they are comfortable about your taking notes. With the list right in front of them, it will seem very natural for you to be writing things down as you cover the different points. Of course you don't want to be tied to the notebook or tablet. You definitely want to make sure you are listening attentively to the customer. Taking notes properly, looking back and forth at the customer as you do that, and using some shorthand in the process will help.

This method also works well on introductory calls if you take the time to first give the general reasons for wanting to see them before covering other more specific areas. If you have done some homework on the company, your list can reflect the follow-up questions you want to ask to fill in the information you need. In fact, when you get into the rhythm of asking questions from the "list," and taking notes, you can often ask detailed questions about topics where purchasing people are often reticent to give information, like volumes and types of products or services being used, or current pricing, or other difficult questions. And, of course, open ended questions are best. If you can get your customer talking, you will learn a lot more. A dialog is much more productive than an interview and more likely to get better results.

Sometimes it is valuable to send the customer an agenda prior to your visit to prepare them ahead of time for what you wish to discuss. For example, if your meeting will be technically oriented, your contact may want his technical people involved. The discussion may involve credit, logistical, or administrative issues so those people may be needed. I'm sure you can visualize other situations where sending an agenda beforehand would be helpful.

Try to bring something that will benefit the customer or prospect to every call. Have a reason for being there.

Remember buyers are trying to solve their problems, not yours. It could be information about a new product, or new information about an old product, that directly affects their business. It could be market information that will make the buyer look good when he or she passes it on to the company's marketing people. Maybe it's public news they haven't seen about a competitor. Maybe it's nothing more than sincere thanks for a recent order. As stressed before, review your sales data and recent information before going in, and have something worth talking about. The customer wants to feel you are on top of his business. Imagine how you would feel if the customer is beaming and comments about the recent large order he or she gave to you and you didn't know about it. That's embarrassing, to say the least.

Occasionally, you can think of things that will demonstrate you are going the "extra mile" to set yourself apart from your competition. Before computers put all the current information about accounts at our fingertips, I used to prepare a comprehensive list of each important account's competitive pricing and leave it with them on the call. The practice was allowed but not encouraged by my company at the time because of the potential for mistakes, but the customers loved the convenience of having the information readily available. I just asked them to realize I was doing it myself and not hang me out to dry if I made an inadvertent mistake. In all the years I did this, I never had a problem with that happening, and it was something the competition was not willing to do.

You can probably think of many things you can do to go the "extra mile" at your accounts. For example, if you see a write-up about your customer in the news or in the trade periodicals, send it to them. It is a great way to keep your name in front of your customer even when you are not there physically. You can also use email to confirm conversations or follow up, or maybe just thank them for an order or something else they have done. You don't want to overdo it, but it can be a powerful "extra mile" differentiation. Be one of those salespeople who is hard-wired with a natural curiosity. Don't always seek to push through your own agenda. Seek to understand your customer's point of view so you can do the "extras" and not just be going through the motions.

When presenting your products or services, be positive.

You'd think that would be obvious, but I can vividly recall listening to a presentation one of our technical people made to one of my major customers. He mentioned several times that our products imparted "fairly decent" properties when used appropriately. He drove me crazy. After the meeting I got him alone and asked him if our products were "good." He said that they were. I told him if I ever heard the words "fairly decent" come out of his mouth again instead of "good" or "excellent" when talking about our products in a presentation to one of our customers, he would no longer be welcome on calls in my territory. On the flip side, it's okay to "spin" a little — in fact, it's necessary to be positive and enthusiastic, but don't "over-spin."

This is a good spot to talk about presentation training. There will be many opportunities for you to make formal presentations, either to your customers or to internal people in your own company. Often you will be using your notebook or tablet for one or two contacts. Or you may be in a conference room where you will be projecting to a larger group of people. Typically you will be using *PowerPoint* or *PREZI* or some other similar presentation software. Make sure your presentation looks professional and offers the information in a straightforward non-complex manner. Practice it enough so that your presentation flows smoothly and be ready to handle the questions you are likely to get after you are finished. Information is readily available in books or on the internet to help you with your skills in this area. Your own company may offer helpful courses as well.

Only promise what you can deliver.

This develops both respect and trust. Sometimes during a call, or a negotiation (which will be covered in more detail in Chapter 14), the customer will ask for something you know your company will not do. When that happens, you need to hold your ground. Be firm, but not dogmatic. Know when to relax your position but realize that in some cases you cannot do what the customer wants. Don't threaten. Do not be confrontational, and do not respond to confrontational people in the same manner. Try to let them talk, and then offer ideas about how to work out the situation within the parameters available.

When the customer is insistent or demanding, it is often better to say you will check and get back to them even if you know you can't offer what they want. This gives the customer time to relax a little before discussing that subject again. And, if you say you'll get back to them, be sure to do that quickly even if the answer is still no. Many customers will try to overpower you. Sometimes you lose their respect if you let them, and you will lose the respect of your management as well. Customers will constantly test your limits. With practice, you will learn how to handle those situations. Thinking through what you can do or say ahead of time will help you prepare. Try to make your learning mistakes (a.k.a. "educational opportunities") when calling on the smaller customers.

Be ready with answers ahead of time to questions customers are likely to ask.

I tried to have short, medium, and detailed answers ready for whatever the situation needed. You need to present these in a non-canned manner tailored to meet the situation. With experience you will learn which "prepared answer" is best and use only enough to satisfy the question. Of course it's good, after doing that, to check by asking if that gave them the information they wanted or needed. If you are new, ask your management or other experienced salespeople to help with this. Sometimes, because of what you are going to cover, you know ahead of time that difficult questions will come up. These questions may involve reasons for a price increase, tightening of credit terms, allocations on specific products, or other issues where the customer will want an explanation. You definitely don't want to be fumbling around at that point. Pricing concerns can be especially big objections or sticking points. If price issues surface when you are selling commodity products, your price may need to be adjusted to be competitive. Or perhaps you offer extra value of some sort that you need to emphasize and sell, so the price becomes reasonable to the customer. If you are selling specialties, either products or services, that the customer cannot get elsewhere, or are better than his alternatives, review the benefits. You will continue to have pricing issues on specialties until the customer agrees your product has important differences and benefits that they are willing to pay for. If questions about pricing come up often, you will need to think of better ways to explain or demonstrate the value of your products or services.

Especially when starting out, you will get questions you haven't considered. Trying to "wing it" at that point usually gets a bad result. It's better to say you don't have the answer but will get back to them quickly. Be sure to follow through promptly by getting those answers and conveying them to your customer. This will, in time, help you to be ready for those questions in the future. You will find that many customers will have the same questions in similar situations, so in a short time you will be able to easily respond in a knowledgeable manner.

Speak kindly about other customers or prospects and competitors.

In general, if you don't have something good to say about someone else or another company, don't say anything. If your customer starts to "badmouth" his competition, don't make any comments, just listen quietly. Your customer may be trying to use you to get information about his competition. If he is expressing displeasure with another supplier, perhaps a competitor of yours, you may learn something about that supplier that will help you avoid similar problems with this customer, or that will help you sell to another customer. Use any opportunity to sell your company without denigrating others. If you talk behind your customers' or competitors' backs, then your clients will assume that you will do the same about them.

Be enthusiastic, optimistic, and happy.

People like to be around enthusiastic, positive people. Brighten their day by your presence. An unconscious habit of mine, when people asked how I was doing, was always to answer, "Excellent." I never really thought about it, but just knew that other folks weren't interested in my problems, and sometimes just by saying "excellent," even if things weren't that good, they seemed better. One time when I responded in my usual manner, my customer laughed. He said he noticed I always said that and thought it was unusual; he liked it. I later decided to put XSELLENT on my car's license plate!

Be creative.

Try to think of a variety of potential solutions for both your customer's and your own needs. Many times, good things will happen. A fresh approach can produce dynamic results. At one point my company faced a situation where we were storing materials in tank cars while waiting for tanks to be built. We were new in that particular part of the business and, as a result, sales were very slow in developing. We were struggling to get a foothold in a market dominated by many other historical suppliers. It was extremely difficult to plan inventory properly because the sales were sporadic. Often we were unable to turn the rail cars around fast enough and had to pay demurrage on them (overtime charges for keeping the rail cars over the time limit). As this began happening frequently, I started calling a few trustworthy potential customers and told them another rail car was coming in so I had to move the material I had on hand right away. I offered them a small discount to the market price on a one-time basis. Since it was a one-time price — which I had been careful to emphasize — it was not really appropriate for them to use it in good faith as a lever with my competition to lower regular ongoing prices. I had to trust them not to do that. This approach was a good deal for both of us. We saved demurrage charges by emptying the rail cars and moving them out more quickly as new rail cars came in, and the prospects lowered their cost on the one ship-ment. In several cases we got our foot in the door for additional busi-ness later because, along with the price, the customers were impressed with our service. Creating new ways to handle situations can pay big rewards. In looking for creative solutions share stories with your team members. You will not know all of the answers. Sometimes someone else in your team has worked with a similar situation and you can ben-efit from that. You can learn a lot from those around you.

Take the appropriate next step forward or ask for the business.

After all, that is the bottom line for why you have worked so hard to put together the kind of win-win relationship where the customer wants to buy from you. That's what has earned you the right to gain the continuing revenue streams that will be coming to your company. Asking for the business or taking the next forward step may take sev-eral different forms. If it is a regular customer, you might want to ask what they see coming in the way of orders so you can keep your people informed. If it is a new or prospective customer, you may need to pro-mote some kind of small beginning, perhaps an initial order for your product or service so they can see how you perform. "Closing the sale" is often handled differently depending on what you are selling and the stage of your relationship with the customer or prospect. If you can't close the sale in an appropriate manner when the timing is right, you will never be successful. Learn what specific successful approaches are best for your products or services when asking the customer to buy. You will have needed to develop enough value in the customer's eyes for them to give you a chance and then closing the sale will be rela-tively easy. When the prospective customer is not ready to buy, several issues may be coming in to play. You may have asked the wrong ques-tions and presented the wrong solution as a result. Perhaps you have asked the right questions but haven't listened to the answers. You may have short cut the presentation or gone through it too quickly and the customer hasn't understood or "absorbed" it. Perhaps you haven't built enough trust so that the customer believes your "claims." Ultimately all of these come down to the fact that they haven't seen enough of the value-benefit/cost relationship, so you will need to work harder on that. Remember, in the absence of value, everything ends up being about price. You want to demonstrate enough value that price becomes a non-issue.

Try to reach some agreement on how to proceed by the end of each call.

I always liked to summarize what we discussed and make sure that both the customer and I understood where we were going in the future. That might include a few simple goals or agreements or detailed major projects. You both need to be on the same page.

When you accomplish your purpose or get the order, thank people for their attention, shake hands, and leave.

I have seen salespeople throw away opportunities they had in their pocket by not knowing when to quit. I can recall a salesperson telling me about spending two weeks preparing for what was expected to be a very tough negotiation with a large customer. As it turned out, five minutes into the meeting she had achieved the desired result. She resisted the inclination to keep selling, thanked the customer and left. As she pointed out to me, her mission was to get the sale, not to make a presentation. That's an important lesson for all salespeople: Ask for the order and then, when you get it, thank people and leave!

If your sales calls are "one time" sales opportunities (like retail, automobiles, insurance, or similar types of selling), many of the tips we mentioned above are still important. The added issue is determining what the customer wants and needs quickly, since you normally don't have much time to establish that. Asking questions initially, and learning as much of this information as you can up front, is very important. Customers appreciate salespeople who do their homework even if it's in a situation where the sales process only takes a relatively short time. When you have a good picture of their needs and desires, and you are offering something that will appeal to them, you are way ahead of the game.

These are just a few suggestions for what to do on your sales calls. I'll cover other ideas when we review the importance of building strong customer relationships. And again, if many of your sales calls employ methods other than personal visits, these ideas are still important for your success.

★ ★ ★ ★ ★
POINTS

- ★ Learn as much as you can during the first few calls
- ★ Be punctual
- ★ Treat everyone you meet with respect
- ★ Make a good first impression
- ★ Have a plan
- ★ Give the customer your full attention
- ★ Respect their time; don't overstay your welcome
- ★ Bring something of value; without value, it's all about price
- ★ Go the "extra mile"
- ★ Always be positive
- ★ Work to improve your presentation skills
- ★ Only promise what you can deliver
- ★ Have responses ready for common questions or situations
- ★ Speak kindly about others
- ★ Be creative
- ★ Share ideas with your team to develop better solutions for your customers
- ★ Summarize the path forward
- ★ Ask for the order or the next forward step
- ★ If the customer is reluctant, review your call for possible errors
- ★ You may need to ask additional questions for clarification or to restate your benefits
- ★ When you have the desired result, thank people and *leave*

CHAPTER 8: HANDLING INFORMATION
How to Gather, Organize &
Make Use of What You've Learned

In the selling process, you will learn a lot of important information about your customers and the markets they serve. The handling and flow of this information is important for several reasons. You are the eyes and ears of your company. Your company must have information about your customers to better satisfy their needs and the needs of others like them in the market. Data from the field will be useful in developing new products, or in making decisions to discontinue current items. Your company needs to know what is going on in the customer's market in order to be ready for new trends or changes. Your company must be aware of market pricing information to adjust prices quickly and effectively in order to remain competitive and possibly increase profitability. You will be sharing your information with other salespeople in your company so they will be more effective. And, of course, you have to retain and remember information you have learned about your customers so you will be able to respond to their needs.

This section will cover the best ways to transmit and retain the information that is developed in the selling process. Formerly, almost everything was transmitted to paper, a very time-consuming process with poor and slow retrieval techniques. In the modern information age, paper is practically obsolete in the selling process. Data and other information can be retained, retrieved, and disseminated much more easily now through various types of electronic media.

Much of the important information needed by your company is dispersed in call reports. Most salespeople hate doing call reports — often because companies try to utilize call reports in ways for which they were not designed, such as tracking call data or numbers of calls per week or month. Some companies insist that the latest, greatest sales techniques be used during the call, and then documented in the call report. That's a waste of the salesperson's valuable time, and they should know that. If the company's sales managers are on the ball at all, these uses of call reports are not needed, and are even counter-productive, because salespeople often waste time bogged down in the reporting process. You may have to work with the call report system your company has established, but if you keep the following thoughts in mind, your reports should be easier to do and will be more useful as a reference.

From the perspective of your company, call reports should be brief, to the point, and accomplish two things: First, call reports should be a record for the salesperson of what is going on at the account, and of what important actions need to be taken by the salesperson or the company as a quick follow-up reference for the next call. Second, reports should include any items that are very important for the salesperson's company to know about the account or market. If you keep those ideas in mind, you will have no problem doing quick and effective call reports. The first part of that is pretty self-evident. The second part may not be.

With smartphones, notebook, and tablet type computers readily available, all the basic data (name, address, phone numbers, contacts, etc.) for a call report on a customer needs to be input only once. After that, each time a call is made, the profile is pulled up and the date and any new contact names are added, along with comments or other appropriate information. Any action or information desired by the customer should be included in the call report. That way, it is easy to determine if any follow-up work is needed before calling again. A good call report shouldn't require more than 15 to 20 minutes of your time. Unfortunately, in many companies, the time it takes to do the administrative work (call reports, expense statements, etc.) is very high, often taking time away from valuable customer contact.

Call reports can be easily attached to emails when important action is needed from other employees. Companies may expect their salespeople to spend hours doing call reports filled with every detail, but often the internal employees who receive them don't bother to read them, or can't remember them or how to retrieve them later when the information is needed. I knew a salesperson who got so disgusted with the fact that no one read his call reports that he included a statement about half-way through one of them offering to buy a drink for anyone who read that far. As I recall, he didn't buy many. Some salespeople end up spending more time doing call reports than making calls. What a waste of talent and time! Knowing that, keep them simple and brief and to the point. If no one reads them, at least you haven't spent much time on the process.

I found it was best to put action items up front, then a synopsis of the most important information (for appropriate management), and finally any additional information I wanted to retain for myself to jog my memory later if needed when dealing with the customer. This is a good format because it gets the important information up front where it is most likely to be read, and isolating action items saves people's time. If you put action items in a call report, it is usually a good idea to follow up with a phone call, email, or text message to the appropriate internal people. Don't expect that you can send the request for action in to your company and someone will automatically see it as their responsibility and respond. Internal follow-up is just as important as following up with customers.

Here is an example of a typical call report:

Sample Call Report

XYZ Corporation
1033 Kings Road
Avenel, NJ 08863

Date of Call: 06/10/13

Author: Lee Davis

Contacts:
Lydia Smith, PhD
       Technical Manager
       Research and Development
       555-826-4111
       lsmith@XYZcorporation.com
Richard Lukas
       Vice President, Sales and Marketing
       555-826-6633
       rlukas@XYZcorporation.com
Subject: Status of TXSS Testing and Market Potential

Action Items: Send an additional 3 liters of TXSS lubricant additive for additional tests to the attention of Lydia Smith at the address above.

Richard has been very busy with their lubricant joint venture with Horgans in Britain. The plant will be producing 20,000 metric tons of specialty lubricants. This is a major play for additional European business.

In regard to TXSS, XYZ Corporation has done more extensive testing and is quite impressed. They plan to test at least three additional lubricants using this additive, and believe if their additional testing continues to look good, there may be at least three markets where this product could fit. Richard would not disclose the specifics of the markets in question. All of this depends on price.

Market 1 — TXSS would be used in a new family of products. This would not be a unique application, because they can do this now with alternate chemistry, but that route is somewhat expensive. This is a major application with some sub applications, and the TXSS potential could reach 10M pounds. Higher probability would be in the 3-5M pound range. This would take 2 to 3 years at least to develop. Their goal is to achieve the higher performance needed in this market at lower cost.

Market 2 — TXSS would be used in a market that XYZ feels they control now. This would be a drop in replacement for an existing product and much quicker to develop. They believe product development and re-qualification would take less than one year. Potential here is 2 to 4M pounds of TXSS which is a lower volume but has a higher probability of success.

Market 3 — This would be European business and would be about 2M pounds.

Total for all three markets (XYZ's potential) would be in the range of 8 to 10M pounds.

All of this is possible in their view if TXSS is priced in the range of "normal" lubricant additives. They don't expect it to be priced low with the standard high volume commodity materials (in the $1.10/lb. range) but feel it must be less than $1.60/lb. to have much chance. They felt that it would have the best potential if it were priced in the high $1.40s or low $1.50s at most. Obviously price will affect potential volumes.

Again, they would like 3 more liters of TXSS lubricant additive for additional testing.

★ ★ ★ ★ ★

This example is probably longer and more detailed than a typical everyday call report, but it gives you the idea about what you are trying to accomplish.

As part of the organizational plan, discussed in Chapter 2, you can set up a file on your computer or device for each area or sector (or company, if I was using the contact call plan). In this file, you should include a profile of the customer and a copy of the latest one or two call reports for each customer. Again, with modern software, which allows notes about previous calls with all the other information, these tasks are much easier. You may want to add a note to your calendar far enough ahead of making the appointment to check that all action items from previous calls have been addressed; this gives you a chance to tend to anything left unfinished, and insures that the results will be available to review with your customer by the next meeting.

It is important to look at the appropriate material along with the latest sales records before the call. In most cases you can do it from wherever you are by connecting your smartphone, notebook or tablet directly to Wi-Fi. If you have the information handy when setting up the appointment, it may give you something to talk about and can also alert you to any unfinished work that needs to be done for the customer before making the call.

The fast, efficient flow of information, both externally and internally, is critical today for a salesperson to be successful. And it doesn't take much time if done correctly and for the right purpose. Many new tools are available, and it is easy and efficient to use cellphones or computers to text information or pictures quickly if needed. There is no excuse for being uninformed about important situations and what course of action is needed.

Learn how to use all these new tools. If you don't, your competition will. However, as much as communicating information is important; don't get bogged down in tons of data and call reports. Remember that your primary job is to be in front of customers and prospects selling your company's products or services. After all, that's why you have a sales job in the first place.

★ ★ ★ ★ ★
POINTS

- ★ You are the eyes and ears of your company
- ★ Information is important to you and your company
- ★ Set up call reports so only new information is needed each time
- ★ Put action items first
- ★ Put company information next
- ★ Put information important to you last
- ★ Incorporate this data into a device which allows fast and easy retrieval
- ★ Review recent call reports before each call
- ★ Even though transmitting information is important, don't forget your primary responsibility is to sell

CHAPTER 9: FOLLOW UP
Immediately Join the Top Twenty Percent!

I can say with confidence that if you master the follow-up aspect of selling, you will be in the top 20 percent of salespeople — even if your other selling skills are a little deficient. This may be the most critical part of selling. Follow-up is something you must do all the time, every time. Always do what you say you will do. Don't make any promises you do not intend to keep. Become excellent at follow-up, and you will be among the elite of salespeople and effective relationships will blossom.

Let's talk about the customer's needs. While making your rounds of calls, the customers will be asking for information, samples, or a variety of other things for many different reasons. Some of these requests will be about products or services they are already buying, and some of them will be to help them make buying decisions. The way you handle these requests will be very important. Amazingly, many salespeople don't follow up at all. As I emphasized, simply following up would probably move you to the top 20 percent immediately. Hopefully, your company is set up so that you can respond and get whatever the customer needs quickly and efficiently. If you must delay for some reason, voice mail or email can relay that information to the customer so they are kept well informed.

What is follow-up? In its simplest form, it is *doing what you say you are going to do — every time.* That means doing anything within your power that the customer wants and making sure they know that you have done it. The customer may want you to get him some price information, literature, a sample, or something similar. Make sure that you do it. If a customer asks you for something you cannot do, make sure they know that you can't do it. Don't leave them with the impression that you will fulfill their request, and then never produce, thinking they will forget — they won't.

All kinds of things are follow-up. You may write them a letter or send an email before the call confirming an appointment, or after the call confirming the discussion and what action items will be taken. You may make a phone call or send an email to follow-up on a sample being tested. Follow-up may simply mean keeping additional people in the loop.

Handle easy requests as if they are routine. In reviewing things you promise to do, it's good to remember the old expression, "It's better to under-promise and over-deliver."

What that means is this: do not set the bar of customer expectations too high. If you are sure you can do what you say you can do, that's great, but if you have any concerns, give yourself some room. Often it's good to set the bar so you can exceed it with room to spare. If you do more than you say you will, the customer will be delighted. If you deliver less than you said you would, even if it is more than would normally be expected, the customer will be disappointed. Don't set yourself up for failure before you begin.

You will find that when you consistently follow up on customer requests, the customer may start counting on you for things that they had to spend considerable time doing before. Your diligence will make their job easier. If the customer is worth the extra effort, you will be cementing a long-term relationship. If not, be sure you are declining their requests in a nice but firm way. Again, don't leave them expecting something they won't get. Only you can be the judge of how much effort each customer or potential customer is worth. If you are unsure of how much time, including follow-up, a customer should get in the beginning, discuss it with your sales manager, who generally has a better idea of the big picture and can guide you in this area. It is usually better to respond to customers more than perhaps seems necessary in the beginning, and then wean them back later if it turns out to be excessive. Remember, your time is valuable, so don't commit yourself to more than you can handle. If you do, other things may start to fall through the cracks, and the results will be the opposite of what you are trying to achieve.

As I mentioned earlier, making sure customers are aware that you followed up is almost as important as doing it. If they have asked you to call on someone else in the company, make sure to let them know you did it. If you sent them some information, ask if they received it. On each call, you can subtly remind them of some follow-up you did. All other things being equal, customers usually give their business to the person who does the best job of following up.

Many salespeople who are selling in situations where it appears there may be only one chance at the sale neglect follow-up. For example, selling automobiles is usually not a long-term selling process. People come in and they buy or they don't. They may do a little comparison shopping or negotiating and then either buy or not. Even in situations like this, follow-up is critical to success in achieving top salesperson status and income. How many automobile salespeople do you think have any idea why they missed a sale? In my experience, very few even try to find out. How can you determine the problem and decide how to do better, unless you check back with the people who did not buy? And for those who *do* buy from you, whether you sell cars, appliances, real estate or services, you need to realize that they will buy again, even if it's sometime in the future. Do you want them to think of you when that happens? Do you want them to refer you to others? Of course you do! How will that occur without some kind of regular follow-up or after-the-sale (or non-sale) contact? It usually won't. Remember that *current* customers are the best *future* customers and the best advertising!

I recall our home-buying process when my wife and I were transferred to the Chicago area. We looked at homes with several realtors in different suburbs of the city. One realtor stood out from the rest because she began with a ton of questions to define our needs and wants (something that is very important if you might only get one chance at the customer). Then she followed up with us at the end of each day, checking back to refine her search criteria by finding out what we did and did not like about the homes she showed us. We eventually bought a home through her, but that was not the end of it. When we moved in she was there with a small gift, thank-you note and even a list (including phone numbers) of businesses, restaurants, attractions and other local places of interest. A month or so later, after we were settled in, she called again to see if everything was still to our satisfaction, and asked if there was anything else we needed where she could help. We got Christmas cards with handwritten notes from her for each of the five years we lived there. I'm sure you can guess who got the listing on our house when we were transferred again and had to sell. This real estate agent was a professional. She did a superb job of taking care of the details and following up during the selling process, just as we expected, because she had done all that during the buying process originally. And in all the job transfers and other moves I was involved in over the years, I never knew another realtor to do such a fine job of follow-up.

Follow-up often will be beneficial to get the sales process moving again. Prospects may leave you with time-worn scenarios like, "I'll look it over and let you know," or, "I'll have to run this by my boss to see how he feels about it," or perhaps, "I need to check with the technical people to see what they think."

These situations can be the kiss of death — unless you learn how to handle them. Some solutions are as simple as asking, on the spot, what parts of the proposal need more explanation. Some situations will require follow-up to see if your prospect actually contacted his people (just as rare an occurrence as salespeople following up). You may need to offer to meet with them and the other people, suggesting that you will be able to cover the information efficiently and they won't have to take the time trying to remember it all. If entertainment is part of your toolbox, you might offer to meet over lunch or dinner, with all the involved parties, to break the logjam. As a last resort, you may have to go around your contact to get to the ultimate decision maker. As we will discuss in Chapter 10, this is tricky, so make sure you have exhausted all other opportunities first.

I cannot emphasize enough that effective follow up will put you among a minority of salespeople using a critical skill. It will work for you ... *guaranteed.*

★ ★ ★ ★ ★
POINTS

- ★ Following up puts you immediately among the top salespeople
- ★ Do what you say you are going to do. Always!
- ★ Under-promise and over-deliver
- ★ Refuse nicely if you can't do something or if the value received is not worth the time
- ★ Follow-up is important even in "one shot" sales opportunities
- ★ Find out why sales (or non-sales) happen
- ★ Make sure the customer is aware you followed up
- ★ Follow up to keep the sales process moving

CHAPTER 10: BUILDING CUSTOMER RELATIONSHIPS
How to Become Your Customer's First Buying Choice

At one time I thought that the growing use of the internet would signal the end of customer relationships. The internet held the promise of getting anything online and eliminating the middleman and all the associated costs. It is true that there are some sales of this type where salespeople are not needed. Companies often hold auctions or solicit quotes over the internet. Purchasing can be done online with no salespeople involved. In spite of that, those situations are still not the norm, and won't be for the foreseeable future. Whenever important high-priced products or services are purchased, quality salespeople and their companies continue to offer extra value through clarifying information, service after the sale, and other benefits that come with a personal relationship.

A considerable amount of my experience was in selling commodity products, and if there were ever materials that would seem to lend themselves to large-volume "faceless" selling, commodities seemed to fit the bill. Many large customers buy all kinds of products over the internet through global product auctions — or something similar like putting products or services out for bid — but they still want the assurance that the majority of their needs are met from someone they know and trust. Whatever the product or service, if repeat business or significant service is involved, and what you offer is critical to *their* business, the customers want to feel they will be taken care of properly. If you have the kind of relationship that assures them of that, and you are relatively competitive, you will get the business. The rest of this chapter is designed to show you how to develop that kind of relationship.

As social beings, nearly all facets of our lives revolve around relationships. If you are willing to master the skills necessary to build and grow relationships, you will enjoy a significant advantage over your "less connected" counterparts. In business, effective relationships can mean the difference between excellence and mediocrity, or between success and failure. In sales, relationships are the cornerstone of success.

Sales relationships fall somewhere on the spectrum between business and personal. No good business relationship is 100 percent business; there needs to be some degree of personal relationship as well. The amount of personal relationship you inject into your sales activities will depend chiefly on your personality and style and those of your customers and prospects. I have worked with excellent salespeople who had strong personal relationships with many of their customers. I have worked with some top salespeople who kept personal relationships to a minimum. However, even those people had some level of personal interaction in their dealings with their customers.

Following are a few ideas to promote your business relationships. Some are critical. All can be effective. Especially try to develop the ones that fit with your strengths, and become proficient enough in the others that your weaknesses are minimized. These ideas will also work well in selling situations that are not face-to-face.

Learn to be sensitive to your customer or prospect.

Determine your customer's personality type and adapt your style to theirs as much as possible. As mentioned previously, if they are bottom line, get-to-the-point types, learn to do it that way. If they are laidback conversationalists, be prepared to go with their flow. Be flexible. Try to be the kind of person they like, but be sure to be genuine. All of us are multi-faceted mixes of personality. Learn to recognize the aspects of your personality that will fit well with those of your various contacts, and emphasize those areas. This does not mean being phony or fake — it means stressing different parts of your personal style with different people. If you can do this, they will look forward to seeing you. Customers enjoy buying from people they like.

Be respected for your professionalism.

Becoming proficient in the use of these relationship-building ideas, and practicing things you've learned from other topics covered in this book, will turn you into a polished professional.

Honesty is critical.

Emphasize the positive, but make the customer aware of any important negatives. This will build trust and respect. Nothing is so important to sell that you intentionally deceive the customer. If you do, it will come back to haunt you and any relationship you have developed will be ruined. In many industries, people move within that industry when they change jobs. You will find them one week at one company and the next week at a competitor. If you are telling stories at one place that don't mesh with what they find out at their new place of employment, your credibility and relationship will be destroyed. Being honest keeps things easy to remember. You don't have to reveal everything you know, but whatever you decide to reveal or discuss should be the truth.

Consistency is very important.

Being consistent builds credibility and trust. Do what you say you will do — every time. It is much easier dealing with a prospect or customer when they know what to expect. They will value consistency, and since many salespeople do not behave consistently, this can be a major edge for you.

Building relationships requires time.

You cannot build strong customer relationships without investing considerable time. Determine if the customer or prospect is worth it, and be willing to make the effort. You have to earn the right to advance. It's a little like dating: every time you meet, look for ways to improve the relationship.

Bring value to the customer.

The people you call on appreciate salespeople who don't waste their time. Value can take many forms, depending on what the customer wants and needs. You can bring them information on the supply or pricing trends in the market. You can keep them up to date on changes taking place with their competitors (excepting, of course, confidential information). With the trend these days of companies having to do more with less, the people you are calling on are frequently overworked. If you can make their job easier, that's a major plus in their perception of you. You are out calling in the market every day and, as a result, you can usually give them important, non-confidential information they don't have time to find out for themselves. This helps them look good to their management. If you regularly supply useful extra information, you can be assured you will continue to be welcome. In addition, the salespeople who are not helping them and bringing added value will not be given much time.

To summarize the value of information: it's important to be knowledgeable about your company's business, your customer's business, your competition, and how it all fits together. You should be doing this on a regular basis anyway — why not use the information you have gathered to become a significant source of knowledge for your customer?

Use all your assets to bring value to the call.

One of our salespeople became the "answer man" for his customer, even on products we did not offer. Needing solutions, the client called our representative — instead of the other company's salesperson — with specific questions. Our excellent technical group could often give him the answers he needed, even on the competitor's products. That kind of time-consuming help had to be given judiciously but, for us, the account was worth the extra time. Granted, that level of assistance may be a little unusual, but you want your customer to think of you first when he has a problem or a question because he believes you can help. Consider being the "answer man" for your most important accounts.

Become an excellent communicator.

Keep people informed. If your contacts aren't involved with something you are doing with others in their company, make sure they are aware of the situation. Relationships can be ruined when people feel they are not being kept "in the loop." Large companies often have multiple locations where the purchasing of some materials or services is controlled corporately and other purchases are controlled at the branch locations. In one instance our salesperson was calling on the corporate purchasing agent at the headquarters of a company with many locations. During the call, she mentioned some successful work our people had done that had solved a major problem at one of the customers' branch locations. As a result of knowing that information, the corporate purchasing agent disclosed a very large requirement that was controlled and purchased by one of the other branch locations. This open communication, which kept the corporate purchasing person fully informed, helped open the door for significant new business previously unknown to our company.

If, for some reason, you need to go "over the head" of your contacts, make sure you can do it in a way which will not irritate them, or it could cause major problems for you in the future. One way is to offer to help explain something to the higher level person, or to include them in a group discussion. Bringing in a member of your management gives you an excellent reason to make contact with someone higher in your customer's organization, without your normal contacts feeling you have gone over their heads. Then, if you are careful during the discussion with the "higher-ups," you may be able to move things in the direction you are seeking without ruffling feathers.

For some accounts it may be important to prepare reports at appropriate time periods (perhaps quarterly or annually) which summarize everything you have worked on together. Encourage your contact to share the report with their organization. This can help solve the problem we just mentioned concerning informing additional important people without irritating your main contact. Of course you can use this approach whether or not that is a problem. You are basically offering an occasional status update that should highlight everything done to move the relationship and the business forward. These periodic reviews will emphasize the value the account is receiving as a result. Sometimes you just have to do your own PR!

Open communication is important.

I once dealt with a problem requiring me to seek help from a person that I did not know very well. He said he would have to check with someone else to see if the problem could be worked out. He mentioned his colleague's name, and since I personally knew her, and it was important for her to be involved to solve the problem, I decided to talk with her directly as well. I was later was accused by the first person of going behind his back, causing him to be quite upset. When I investigated the source of his anger, I found out that he had not really wanted to help in the first place but didn't want to offend me by saying so. He had no intention of checking with the friend I later talked with; he just wanted the issue to disappear. My actions had exposed his position in a bad light and he was very irritated about that. In reviewing the situation, I believe more discussion between us up front would have made the situation clearer. I would have realized he was reluctant to become involved and, even though the solution would have been more difficult, the unpleasantness may have been avoided. Open, clear communication is almost always the best approach. Unclear, misunderstood, or otherwise poor communication can cause serious problems.

Learn to be a good listener.

Give the customer or prospect a chance to talk. Most people like to talk, and it helps put them at ease. Put some energy into the listening process. Make sure your facial expressions reflect the fact that you are paying attention. Be sure you understand their position before presenting your point of view. A good way to do this is to ask a few clarifying questions which show you have been listening and indicate that you value their ideas. Many times, just restating their position lets them know you understand. Defuse unpleasant situations by allowing upset customers to express their anger or frustration. If you have trouble in this area, pick up one of several books available on listening skills and practice with a friend until it becomes second nature (see Appendix II). Remember to make eye contact with people when culturally appropriate as you talk and listen. It builds trust. Being able to "connect" with people is very important. Some people can do it naturally; for others, it must be learned. It's very difficult to fake this successfully. If people feel that you are genuinely interested in them and in what they are saying, you are doing it right.

Sincerely compliment your contacts.

It is especially helpful to do this in front of those higher in the organization. Notice the things they do that you like and give them positive reinforcement—it pays huge dividends. Everyone likes a sincere compliment, and people love looking good in front of their boss!

Go beyond the "Golden Rule."

Instead, *do unto others as they want to have done to them.* Be kinder and more helpful than necessary.

Ask questions, lots of them, especially in the beginning.

And take notes. This is a good way to find out about your customer's business. It gets the customers talking and opens doors for other discussions. Later, you will be using questions to clarify opportunities, solve problems, or identify approaches to a myriad of other situations. Incidentally, by asking questions of customers, you will often learn new things about the features and benefits of your own products and how they are used by your customers, which can augment your own company's literature and training programs.

I can recall one time when we were promoting a product, to be used at 100% purity in a coating, for minimizing water blistering on the bottoms of fiberglass boats. Unfortunately, our material didn't seem to be making the progress our company felt it should. When I asked one of our largest customers about how he used it, he told me that our product gave better results in a 70% ratio with another company's product than it did when used at 100%. It turned out that our own lab knew that, but hadn't felt it was important and didn't want to help sell the 30% portion of a competitor's product. When these facts were openly discussed, and we started promoting our product in the blend, sales increased substantially as the blended product became the industry standard.

Learn to be a good conversationalist.

Stay informed on current topics. Learn some trivia. Be interesting to talk to, but tread lightly around controversial topics like politics and religion. Be quick on your feet and inventive in conversations. Learn the art of keeping a conversation going without being knowledgeable on the subject. I can recall having to do this early in my sales career when I was transferred to Kansas City and began covering the Midwest. I found out the main topic of conversation in Nebraska was the football team. That was not uncommon considering the Cornhuskers' success at the time, and the lack of other major sports teams in the area. Since I was new in the area, I knew nothing about the Cornhuskers, or the Missouri Tigers, or any of the rest of the Midwest's favorite teams. I found out that it was easy during the discussion of some excellent game or great play to say something like, "I didn't see that…tell me about it."

Often the customer would begin expounding and conversation became easier. When I'd been there for a while and knew enough to carry on a discussion about those kinds of subjects, I no longer needed to take that approach. Keep in mind that the customer wants to talk about their interests, so listen carefully and, in time, you will learn. Being a good listener can be ranked as one of the most important selling skills you will need to be successful.

It helps to be curious about people. Always look for things of interest and value to others. Observe their office setting and notice what they have displayed. Family photographs, trophies, wall hangings, and other personal items provide valuable clues to your customer's interests and priorities. Sometimes the areas of the country (or world) where they grew up can give you insights and generate interesting conversations. I was playing golf one time with a customer I had just met for the first time who was of East Indian descent and I mentioned how much I enjoyed Indian food. He promptly invited my wife and me to join him and his wife at his favorite Indian restaurant where we had a wonderful evening and got better acquainted. Be aware of these kinds of cultural differences. One salesperson had several clients who were Muslims, and so he would send them cards for Ramadan. They appreciated the gesture and, as no one else was doing that, it helped him develop relationships that encouraged business at some of those accounts. When I was calling in the Northeast, several of my customers were Jewish. I was careful not to send them Christmas cards but sent Happy Holiday cards instead. Little things to be sure, but being sensitive to your clients' differences is important none the less.

Pay close attention to your clients' interests and activities. If they mention they are going to play in a golf tournament or run a marathon, or engage in some other interesting pursuit, be sure to record that in your calendar or in your follow-up notes so you won't forget to bring it up later. They will be impressed that you remembered and you will enjoy hearing about the results. This kind of attention to detail is important in helping to develop the connections we discussed earlier.

You will also find many contacts who share your interests. That will make it even easier, as you will have common areas to talk about. One of my enduring interests is sailing. During my tenure as a sales manager, I learned that the president of one of our major accounts owned a 55-foot sailboat. His wife didn't enjoy sailing at all, so he was always enthusiastic about finding other people to take out on his boat with him.

When we became acquainted, he invited our salesperson and me for a day on the water. After sailing in the ocean off the coast of New Jersey for several hours, he tried to start the motor for our return trip through a narrow canal back to the marina. Unfortunately, we found the battery was dead and the motor wouldn't start. He turned the helm over to me and I sailed up and down for an hour or so in the open water, where a motor wasn't necessary. Meanwhile, he got on the radio and arranged for a tow. We became fast friends and our salesperson was able to develop a relationship with an upper-level contact he barely knew before that event. Common interests and a little serendipity can sometimes work wonders.

Be alert for unusual opportunities.

One large company's CEO, Michael, invited the CEO of their most important customer, Taylor, to be his guest in a VIP box at a New Year's Day College Football Bowl game between the top two teams that year. Unfortunately, Michael did not think to invite his own company's corporate account manager, Carol — who was their "person on the ground" responsible for that important account — to join them. After learning about the upcoming game, Carol convinced her management to get tickets so she could also attend the game with her customer. She then talked with her top contacts at the customer so they understood she would be included. Since Carol lived in the area of the country where the account was located, one of her customer contacts even arranged for her to fly down and back to the football game on the customer's corporate jet. Carol ended up being able to spend several hours traveling back and forth to the game talking with Taylor (the customer's CEO), a high-level contact she had never met. Talk about an opportunity! This turned out to be a great way to build a more in-depth relationship with a major customer (and she also had the opportunity during the event to impress Michael, her own company's CEO, with how well she was handling the account). Recognize the limits, but develop a feel for when you, like Carol, may need to assert yourself in situations where you should be involved.

Handle problems properly and promptly.

Be sure to use problems or complaints as opportunities to build relationships. If you solve a problem promptly and satisfactorily, your relationship can be stronger than before. Usually it's not the actual problems which cause difficulty in relationships; it's more often the ways we respond to the problems. Sometimes salespeople procrastinate, don't take problems seriously, or take the wrong actions. Strong relationships are often built on the way we handle adversity. Because it's so important, we'll spend more time on handling complaints or problems in Chapter 15.

While we are on the subject of relationships, become aware of strong relationships that already exist between your customers and some of your competitors. One of our salespeople mistakenly made the assumption that, because he had most of the business on one group of products, his customer would be interested in buying a different group of products from him as well. He worked very hard to offer special incentives and other packages to get something started on that second group, only to find that his contact immediately passed the details of his various offers to the competitor. As is often the case in those situations, the customer had a strong historical relationship on that specific group of products with the competitor, and just used the salesperson's activity as a way to get a better deal on those items from his major supplier. This illustration points out one of the cardinal sins of selling, which is to lower the price and not get the business. If you are going to upset the market, you better be sure you are going to get good results for doing it.

Many times you will be on the other side of this equation and, because of your excellent relationships, you will be getting information allowing you to retain business in response to activities by your competitor. Unfortunately, when competition gets active, the prices and profit margins usually end up lower than before. This is a good time to mention that it is useful to know the characteristics of the salespeople you are competing against. Are they top salespeople or journeymen? Are they likely to try to "buy" business by constantly trying to sell on price? The better you know your competitors the easier it is to anticipate problems and also take advantage of weaknesses that may be there.

With new products or services, salespeople typically try to sell the largest potential customers first and then trust that the smaller customers in the industry will follow suit in order not to be left behind. That approach is usually the best way to get the most "bang for the buck" when introducing something that's "new or improved." If you have the relationships to get a proper hearing, and the large customers are still not buying, try the process in reverse. Sometimes by selling a smaller customer or two, the large ones will notice the increased competition and be drawn to your product or service in spite of their initial reluctance. One salesperson spent over a year trying to sell a major customer a new product, with no results. He finally took it to a smaller account, and within 6 months they had it in a commercial material. Faced with the competition of this new product in the market from someone a fraction of their size, within one year the large customer started buying the product as well.

As important as customer relationships are to the selling process, don't ever get lulled into thinking they will make up for sloppy salesmanship. You still have to review your sales figures, ask about business, review pricing, bring value, and make sure everything else is carefully handled. A salesperson I knew named Bill told me about a customer, Richard, with whom he had an incredible relationship. He had about eighty percent of Richard's business on one product and about sixty percent of his business on another. Richard's company was Bill's largest customer. He took Richard to lunch every month, with a standing appointment. Bill and Richard and their wives went to dinner together about once a quarter. The families took vacations together occasionally. It couldn't have been better. However, during one time period Bill noticed that Richard's business was slowly dropping off. He assumed that Richard's company's overall business was down, until finally it got so bad that he asked about the situation. Richard calmly pointed out that Bill had not been keeping him competitive, and that other offers were better so he took them. Bill looked at Richard and said, "But Richard, I thought we were friends." Richard leaned over to Bill and said, "Bill, we *are* friends, but this is *business.*"

Don't ever forget you are in business and, even after building the important customer relationships, make sure you are doing the rest of your job properly.

As you can see, strong customer relationships are still extremely important. If you have a pleasant personality and are willing to work at it, they are usually not hard to develop. These connections, combined with solid salesmanship, will help every salesperson achieve excellent results.

★ ★ ★ ★ ★
POINTS

- ★ Salespeople still supply added value to customers
- ★ Relationships are critical
- ★ Adapt to your customer's personality, culture, and style of working
- ★ Honesty and consistency are essential; they build respect and trust
- ★ Be willing to invest an appropriate amount of time
- ★ Use what you know to make the customer's job easier
- ★ Become a good listener
- ★ Look for opportunities to compliment others sincerely
- ★ Keep people "in the loop"
- ★ Be very careful about "going over someone's head"
- ★ Open, clear communications are usually best
- ★ Ask questions; sometimes your customers know your product better than you do
- ★ Learn techniques to keep the conversation going
- ★ Look for areas of common interest
- ★ Be alert for situations where you need to be involved
- ★ Understand the customer's relationships with competitors
- ★ Sometimes it's better to sell smaller customers first
- ★ Even with a great relationship, don't take business for granted

CHAPTER 11: SELLING INTERNALLY
Building Your Inside Team

The key to success with a customer is frequently based on selling your *own* company on your proposed course of action to get or keep the business. This may include meeting a competitive price, allowing some special terms, or doing something else that may be out of the ordinary. I have found that internal selling is every bit as important as selling the customer, and sometimes can be much harder. Here are some ideas that should help.

Building relationships with your own people, just like building relationships with customers, is essential to your success. Start networking within your own company. Ask yourself, "Do I know where or who to go to or call when I need something specific done?" If not, get busy finding out who does what. Be aware of what I call the "network of competence," that is, the people who are competent and get things done, and how they relate to each other. This is often different from the formal network of authority. For example, one salesperson told me that if they wanted something done in the lab, they would call the production manager, rather than the lab manager, who was their official resource but was often unresponsive. It is important to understand who approves your requests, including all the facilitators in between, and especially work on those relationships. I had to learn this the hard way. When I was a new, young salesperson, I was having real trouble getting people in my own company to do things for me. Requests would be pushed aside, become inactive, or simply get turned down. When the sales director was traveling with me on one occasion, I asked him about that issue.

He told me that the company was very impressed with the way I worked with the customers, as sales in my territory had grown impressively. Unfortunately, they were less impressed with how I worked with my own people. I told him I felt my job was selling customers and I was doing it well, and their jobs were to handle the internal support, which I expected them to do properly. He pointed out that you "catch more flies with honey than with vinegar," and that my requests were just a few of many that the overworked internal group had to handle. He made the suggestion that if I would take the time to treat them like I treated the customers, I would see much better results.

I decided to change my ways. Instead of complaining and pushing when something was late or not done at all, I started to notice the requests that were done fast and correctly. I then sent sincere compliments to the people involved. I would send copies of the kudos to their supervisors when appropriate. I started looking for good things to compliment. Instead of being lost on the bottom of their stacks, almost overnight my work started getting moved to the top. Inside people became receptive to my requests. The difference was obvious, and it wouldn't have happened had I not learned to build those internal relationships. While I admit I initially began this technique to advance my own programs and requests, I found that my appreciation for those who helped me grew and created genuine relationships. Try it — it will work wonders.

Trying to sell your people on a complicated course of action usually takes some kind of written communication or memo proposing your recommendations. If you decide to work on a proposal this way, you may need to follow up with a phone call or two to make sure your plan is moving through the pipeline. In the process, it's important that your facts are accurate and you are scrupulously honest in their presentation. If you get a reputation for stretching the truth, your requests or ideas will not be taken seriously. If your marketing people meet a competitive price for you, only to find out later the price was incorrect — and the whole market dropped and became less profitable as a result of how they responded to the information you gave them — they will be very reluctant to trust you again. If you are not sure if the customer is telling the truth, make sure your people know that. Maybe they have seen activity elsewhere in the market and can help you determine the real situation.

You will know your customers pretty well over time. You will find some are honest and straightforward, and others less so. You can then be the judge of the next steps in talking with your own people. I remember that one of our salespeople put a note on the bottom of a competitive price document for a particular customer who was known for fudging the facts occasionally. The note read, "I think he was telling the truth this time!"

As you develop a reputation for being honest and competent with your inside people, you will be amazed at the results. They may start coming to you as an expert in one area or another. At one point in my career, I was selling to a very large market in the Chicago area which tended to be a geographic price leader for the total US market. When competitive prices started popping up in other parts of the country, the product managers came to me to verify that similar things were going on in Chicago to determine whether or not to take action. A history of competence and honesty, and being in the right place, had made me the go-to guy in some of these situations. Just being in that position in many cases made my internal selling job easier.

When trying to sell your company on doing something differently, you may run into the "tribal knowledge" trap. Tribal knowledge is a term often referred to as knowledge "known yet undocumented," such as information that has been handed down from generation to generation with no specifics to refer to in place. It is knowledge contained within a group that is assumed to be correct and useful, but has no known data or analysis to verify that this is the case; things have just always been done that way. Salespeople may inherit accounts where the previous salesperson — and perhaps many in the company — are unwilling to change procedures or processes that have been going on for a long time. They may think the customer won't stand for it or will become irritated, or perhaps they believe "the way we are doing it is the way it has to be done," or, as noted, "that's the way we have always done it." Sometimes it's just the fact that it's hard to overcome the inertia of the status quo to actually make changes that may be needed. It's a good idea to test preconceived ideas occasionally. They often turn out to be right, but I have found that, at times, they are not. Maybe the situation has changed or the information the current approach is based upon is flawed. Perhaps the people have changed and old taboos are no longer applicable.

Don't be afraid to question things that don't seem to make sense. There is a story about a young wife who always cut off the end of the ham before baking it. When her husband questioned her about it, she said that was what her grandmother and mother had done. At the next family gathering, the husband asked his wife's grandmother why she did it that way; the grandmother replied that she had to cut it to make it fit her roasting pan! Sometimes the pan size has changed, but everyone is still cutting off the end of the ham.

How do you get people to consider changes or new ideas? Sometimes, depending on the personalities involved, you have to float the idea, offer the potential positive results, and stand back to give them time to think about it. It's obviously important for the people involved in the change to be on board, or it won't be implemented very well or at all. We realized this effect when we started "bundling" products and services together for the first time. That approach was a major change for both us and the customers. It had never been done that way before. Resistance was high. We worked hard selling internally (and to the customers), showing everyone that the idea made sense logistically in terms of shipping, and would result in considerable savings for both parties. We started off slowly with just a few items and proved the case. When everyone recognized all the advantages, the concept took off quickly, the customers liked it, and significant extra business resulted from the new process.

Internal selling is extremely important—I can't emphasize that enough. However, it can be very difficult. We tend to take our own people for granted and expect them to do their jobs with no additional respect or consideration. Many salespeople who are very good with customers fall into this trap. Don't let that become part of your internal reputation. Work as hard at internal selling as you do in selling the customers. It's the right thing to do...and it will pay big dividends.

★ ★ ★ ★ ★
POINTS

★ Internal selling is often as important as selling the customers
★ Build internal relationships, up and down the line
★ Look for opportunities to compliment sincerely the inside people who help
★ Send "kudo notes" to supervisors describing ways in which their employees have been particularly helpful
★ Be scrupulously honest when making requests for internal help
★ Don't be afraid to question things that don't seem to make sense
★ Sometimes you have to "float" good ideas for a while and give people time to think about them
★ Sell everyone involved into getting on board before making the changes

CHAPTER 12: CALLING IN DEPTH
Using Management Effectively

The practice of calling in depth refers to the process of developing multiple contacts within your client's organization so you will still be connected if your primary contact is transferred or moves to another company. Some of these people will be "up the line" from your normal contact which may give you a more powerful audience as part of your selling process. Some will be in other parts of the company, perhaps technical or R & D, which help your influence on their product or service selection. By calling in depth and continuing to add contacts, you will not necessarily be subject to the decisions of only one person as you attempt to develop or increase business. Calling with management and others on your team will greatly enhance your ability to call in depth.

As noted previously, the benefits of calling with management are vital to your success. Your management people can help you improve your selling skills. They can help with continuity at the account when you are new. They can help you develop relationships with higher-level people at the customer's location whom you might not have been able to reach on your own. These kinds of relationships can pay big dividends when negotiations are needed or problems occur. And if your management sees you in action doing a great job, they can positively influence the progress of your career!

To do all this, the calls must be properly put together. You must discuss the plan for each call with management, and often with the customer or prospect, ahead of time so everyone understands what is expected.

Let's begin with one very important item. On occasion, you may consider bringing in management for a high level visit or to help defuse a major problem. If you decide to do this, make sure you don't end up raising the conflict to a new level. I have seen business with major customers go right down the drain at high level meetings. My experience is that an ego clash between a customer's top management and your company's top management is never a winning situation. One salesperson I know said his CEO seemed to be more interested in being perceived as the "top dog" than in getting business, which caused several customer relationships to fall apart. It got to the point the salesperson would not schedule him to visit accounts where he thought the personalities involved would clash. Always be aware of the character and temperament of people you are working with from your own and your clients' companies, beware of potential pitfalls, and do your best to facilitate management meetings that will be productive as opposed to confrontational. Fortunately, bad situations are rare — but they do happen. Talking with other salespeople in your company about their experiences calling with specific management people will help you maximize the success of those calls.

If you initiate the activity and want a management person to call with you, send a written communication outlining a plan for the visit to the account. Include a summary about the customer and his business. Tell your management how the customer fits into what you are trying to achieve and how you want them to help you. It's important for management to know what message they should be helping you to deliver. If they initiated the request to call with you, make sure you understand their objectives ahead of time and what is expected of you. It's also a good idea, when talking with the customer about the meeting with your management — no matter who initiated it — to review the goals that are expected to be accomplished. It's a lot easier when everyone is looking at the same agenda. In any case, it is useful to review again what is planned for each call before actually going in. Often this requires more time for complex or very important customers where, in some cases, you might need to send a memo to management ahead of time. Sometimes it is as simple as talking it over in the car while driving to the account.

While we are talking about driving to the account, be sure you know how to get to the customer's location from all directions and, if needed, make a dry run. One time, as his sales manager, I asked a salesperson to pick me up from the airport and, because he had never taken that route to a particular customer's plant, he got lost. We finally found our way, but I pointed out that, had he been traveling with someone at the vice president level or higher, with a low tolerance for delay, they might not have been as understanding. The use of a GPS (Global Positioning System) is an invaluable tool for a salesperson that is driving in unfamiliar territory. You may even want to print out the directions and review them before your trip, in case satellites are unavailable or the GPS quits functioning. Many rental cars have GPS systems available for calling in places where you are flying in and out and are not familiar with the area.

If you have management people who understand selling, have been excellent salespeople themselves, and connect well with your customers, you are fortunate. If not, you need to proceed with caution.

Let me give you a couple of examples from my own experience. Early in my career, I was assigned a sales territory with a very large potential customer. We had been calling on this company and doing technical service work for years, trying to establish a relationship. I asked for management assistance to see if we could crack open the door a little. Janet, a creative and talented assistant director of marketing, agreed to call with me on the president of the prospective customer. Imagine my feelings when, after the get-acquainted "small talk," Janet sat back and said to the president of this company, "John, we've decided to stop calling on your company."

John, surprised, looked at her and said, "So what? Tell me why I should care."

In reply, Janet proceeded to open a large box she had brought with her. From it, she produced a stack of technical service reports about a foot high, and set them on John's desk.

"First, this is the technical service work we have done for your company over the last two years. I'm assuming some of this has been helpful or your technical people wouldn't have continued asking for it. If we quit calling, all that service is gone.

"Second, as one of the top suppliers in our industry, we have been providing your purchasing people market and pricing information which I'm sure has been useful in dealing with your current suppliers.

You need to know what's going on in this industry, and by shutting us out, you will not get the full picture. If we do not finally get some return on our investment, and we quit calling, all of that disappears as well. Is that really what you want?"

It was very quiet for a few minutes. As a new salesperson I figured we'd lost any chance. This was the biggest potential account in my relatively new territory. Bummer!

Finally, John replied, "No, I see your point — that's not what we want. We need to do at least some business with you, and then we'll see how it goes and where you might fit in."

It might not have worked, but we had nothing to lose at that point. And, if you have nothing to lose, you might as well try a bold approach. The important thing was that Janet understood sales, and what was important, and how to use it. It is essential to know your own management people well enough to realize who is skillful enough to be of real help.

Later, when we were doing business with this same company, I was calling on their corporate purchasing manager, Harold. He was quite a bit older than I was, and a more formal type of person, and partially as a result of our differences, building the relationship was going slowly. For this situation, I decided to bring in Robert, one of our vice presidents, to help break the ice.

Harold suggested I make a reservation at one of the top restaurants in Kansas City. This particular restaurant served fresh lobster, which Harold expressed he especially enjoyed, and which was something not readily available then in the Midwest. At that point in my life the only lobster I had ever eaten was a frozen grocery store lobster tail my wife steamed for our first anniversary. I was inexperienced, to say the least.

I picked up Robert at the airport and filled him in on the dinner plans with Harold, a person he had not met before. He commented that he wasn't a big fan of lobster and would normally prefer a steak, but he would try to "go with the flow." At the restaurant, Robert asked Harold about several menu items and Harold commented that lobster was the restaurant's specialty and that the three-pound size was excellent. Harold then ordered the big one and Robert and I did the same. When the lobsters were brought to our table, they were so large they hung off the plates. It was obvious to Harold that I was inexperienced at dismembering a lobster, so he proceeded to teach me in great detail how to eat one, a task he relished. We all enjoyed a great evening. Harold never had a clue that lobster wasn't Robert's favorite meal. On the way back to the motel, Robert mentioned that he would have a hard time sleeping after a dinner that rich, but the experience and the relationship it started was certainly worth it. Harold, the corporate purchasing manager, started taking me under his wing (which I, of course, encouraged), and little by little we developed a great relationship and enough business that Harold's company became my largest customer. Robert, our vice president, not only knew sales, he knew how to relate to people. I learned a lot from working with him.

Then there was the opposite situation. A few years later, at the same customer, Harold had retired and Wes was now their corporate purchasing manager. Our division sales manager, Ted, wanted to meet Wes because this company had now become a very large and important customer. I had met and worked with Wes before he replaced Harold and by this time we had developed a very good relationship (remember the importance of calling in depth in case your primary contact moves on). We often had lunches together, dinners with our wives and, on other occasions, with different management people. Ted and I picked Wes up from his plant after work and headed out for an enjoyable evening. After dinner, Ted mentioned to Wes that he had noticed some "gentlemen's clubs" near downtown and wondered if he would like to go to one. This suggestion came without any prior consultation with me and with no clue about Wes's feelings about this sort of entertainment. Wes looked pointedly at Ted, and responded, "Ted, I've never been to one of those places and I don't plan to start now!"

It was a little uncomfortable for a second or two until I made the suggestion that instead we go over to a local country music club — I had been there with Wes before and knew that was one of his favorite places. Everyone seemed to be having a good time there until about 10:00 p.m., when Ted leaned over to me and mentioned quietly that it was getting late and we needed to be on our way. I explained that Wes seemed to be enjoying himself and, based on past experience, he would be ready to leave in about a half hour or so. Ted didn't want to wait that long so, again without consulting me, he decided to broach the subject himself hoping that Wes would be ready to leave sooner.

After waiting a few minutes, Ted leaned across the table and said, "Wes, we're getting ready to go; do you want to come with us or get a cab?"

Wes gave me an interesting look, and said, "No, I'll go with you guys."

After dropping Wes off at his plant so he could get his car, I drove Ted back to his hotel. On the way, he mentioned how well the evening went. He didn't have a clue. The next time I called on Wes, he was very clear that he didn't care much for Ted. He made the statement that if I ever brought Ted back in, I could kiss much of my business good-bye.

Several months later when Ted decided to schedule some more calls with me, he wanted to go back and see his "good buddy," Wes. I decided not to risk calling Wes with this idea. I just waited a few days and called Ted back, explaining that Wes was going to be unavailable during the week of our calls, and we'd just have to see other customers.

If you are in sales very long, you will have both types of management. Most have been promoted to their position because of solid continuing performance and strong abilities, but there will be a few others who seem to have lost track of their sales skills along the way. As I gained experience, I learned how to minimize the chances for these problems to occur. In the beginning, if a manager wants to travel with you, I suggest you ask other experienced salespeople in your company if they have any tips for you about working effectively with this manager in the field. Sometimes, from your own efforts to sell ideas internally, you will already have learned about the personalities and capabilities of your management people and how effective these different people can be. Most people in management are excellent and can really help you. You may feel like you are walking a tightrope occasionally, as management usually has a major effect on your career, but only you can decide what course of action is best in each case. Stay alert as you work with others. Be aware that situations may not work out as you expected and that, occasionally, you might need to figure out an alternate plan.

For example, you may find that you and one of your managers have different styles, and he or she may want to change your approach to selling in a way that may not work for you personally. I worked for a sales manager who was factual, quiet and methodical, whereas I was more enthusiastic, outgoing, and talkative. When we traveled together, he told me that he thought a lot of what I said did not register with the customers because I covered the information too quickly. However, it was apparent they liked my enthusiasm, which worked with my personality to help me sell. But you can learn from everyone, even those with major differences. From this manager, I learned to be more aware of the need to present information in different ways on occasion, and to allow the customers to respond more often so I could see if what I was saying was being processed. These were valuable lessons for me. Be attentive to learning tips from other people. You will profit from examining what works for them, and from assessing and shoring up areas where you can improve.

Along with good sales results, management interface is very important to your career. If you're good, and they are as well, the synergy can be great. If they are not very good or helpful, as happens occasionally, try to make sure (without hurting your career) that situations where they do more harm than help are very infrequent or never happen.

★ ★ ★ ★ ★
POINTS

- ★ Calls with management, if used properly, can really help you
- ★ Watch out for ego contests — don't make bad situations worse
- ★ Isolate your ineffective managers as effectively, and unobtrusively, as possible
- ★ Take full advantage of your best management people whenever you can
- ★ Make sure your assisting managers know what you are trying to accomplish
- ★ Ask for help from management people who have the right skills to assist
- ★ Be positive— you can learn something from everyone's style of working
- ★ Don't forget to involve others on your team when appropriate

CHAPTER 13: TECHNOLOGY
New Technology for New Techniques

Although we cover much of this material in other parts of the book, technology is such a fast-growing area I wanted to emphasize some of these ideas in a separate chapter. The benefits in using technology to increase your sales effectiveness are extremely impressive. You are no longer limited to the items you have laboriously written down either during the calls or afterwards. You can have notes, sales records, and all kinds of other data available at your fingertips on all kinds of devices like small notebook computers, tablets, and smartphones.

Communication with your office or customers can be instantaneous with these devices. After a relationship with a customer is developed, the possibilities for growing the relationship through more efficient communication are endless. A big part of this is email — information can be sent and viewed at times convenient for both parties, eliminating "phone tag" situations. Email is a marvelous convenience, but be careful. Before you push the "send" button, take a moment to re-read your message. Make sure your sentences are clear and that they communicate your message clearly and politely. Check your spelling, and make certain you are sending your message to the person, or to all the people, you intend to include. It is extremely important to note and be aware that generally you have no control over emails, once they leave your system. They can be forwarded to other people and stored and accessed forever, so make sure you and your company are well represented. Not being careful enough with emails can cause many serious problems both in business and personal affairs.

Many salespeople at the customer's requests now use *Skype, Face Time, Google Talk,* or similar programs, in place of some personal calls.

This is about as close as you can get to actually being there in person, while calling from somewhere else. The customers like the ease and convenience and it is a lot easier on your sales budget. Setting up virtual meetings — where many participants are connected from different places via computer — can also be very effective. Virtual meetings are much easier and less expensive than trying to get everyone together in one geographic location at the same time, which, with everyone's busy schedules, can be very difficult to arrange.

One type of communication like this is the webinar. Webinars are primarily information disseminating tools. People can call from anywhere in the world, log in, view a digital presentation, and ask questions or offer comments via the internet. This is especially good for offering new information to prospects or current customers where the initial cost to make face-to-face calls is prohibitive. You can then use the responses to gauge interest. I have done this with one company at a time, and also with a group of companies in the same industry, where the information presented applied to them all. Questions from the different company attendees were handled confidentially through text messages during the webinar. They are not always set up like that so, if customers are unsure and are unwilling to ask many questions (which is often the case), you can talk with each company individually at a later time to get their feedback and to give them any additional information they want. The responses obtained can also help your company decide whether to invest additional resources in trying to sell to that company or within that industry.

I once put together a webinar from my office in the United States which included company personnel based in Canada and in Singapore. Imagine what it would have cost, in time and money, to bring together a face-to-face meeting with that group of people! Webinars are also very useful in exposing current customers to information available from experts in your company (like technical representatives, for example) without the expense and time involved in sending your company representatives in person.

Technological options are becoming available at lightning speed. For example, new CRM (Customer Relationship Management) software offerings, like those from *Salesforce.com*, are typically totally integrated cloud-based operational efficiency CRM software systems that impact almost every facet of the selling process. These often include back-office systems such as accounting and ERP (Enterprise Resource Planning) software which can integrate internal and external management information across an entire organization.

Many on-demand companies offering software of similar scope include *NetSuite*; *Microsoft CRM* (Dynamics CRM Online), with its application development platforms; SAP's *Business ByDesign*, with its Software Development Kit (SDK); *SugarCRM, Campaigner CRM* and several others. The landscape around these types of applications is becoming very crowded and this will be an exciting growth area in the future. These tools allow you to communicate with your customers and your own company more effectively and efficiently, and may supercharge your sales efforts. Make it part of your routine to explore new developments and to learn how to use them.

★ ★ ★ ★ ★
P O I N T S

★ Stay on top of current technology
★ Be proactive and think of ways technology can help you communicate and disseminate information in a more timely and cost-effective manner
★ Email communication is very powerful, but check emails carefully before sending to make sure they only go to the people you want and say what you planned in the way you planned to say it
★ Search online and check with other salespeople to learn how people are using new technological approaches
★ Be the driver and decision-maker if possible in using or coordinating new technological approaches or possibilities with your customers

CHAPTER 14: NEGOTIATION
Don't Give the Store Away!

In your sales career, you will be faced with opportunities or situations where negotiation is called for. You may be putting a deal together, working out a solution to a problem, or something will come up that highlights a difference of opinion between you and your customer which needs to be resolved. Negotiations may involve something as simple as a discussion of whether or not you need to meet a competitive price for a future or current sale. They may be as complex as working out a major business deal, or a contract involving long-range pricing, terms, and many other parameters for different products or services.

There are many excellent books available to help you specifically with negotiation, some of which I have listed in Appendix II. These books involve complex situations and detailed methods. However, most salespeople will benefit substantially from a few fundamental tips that can help you get started.

In the beginning, it is important to establish agreement to the basic facts of the situation. If you cannot agree on the facts, going forward is usually futile, because everyone is looking at a different picture. During negotiations, try to identify any shared interests. By confirming the shared interests and facts, you have established an excellent place to start. Here is where completely understanding the other party's positions and interests is so valuable. You can do this by asking clarifying questions or seeking additional details or information. Even though you do not agree, and let them know that, it can help to restate the other party's interests so they can see you really do understand their viewpoint. When the customer realizes that you fully understand their situation and interests, they are much more likely to work to understand yours. Excellent communication is the key to good negotiating. Good listening skills are very important to prevent misunderstandings and clarify issues. If possible, after understanding the customer's position, it's much better — if you can — to cast yourself and your customer on the same side of the problem looking for a mutually acceptable solution.

People develop positions based on underlying interests. Some of these positions can be very difficult to deal with because they may end up being sticking points and the parties become closed to other possibilities. Repeatedly verbalizing and stressing the same points by either party tends to "harden" negotiations. Try to avoid going in that direction if at all possible. If someone becomes adamant and keeps returning to previous issues, you may be able to step back a little — try to reach agreement on the underlying broader goals of the negotiation to change the focus of the discussion, and perhaps a better solution will be clearer and those interests can be satisfied with a different approach or solution. I recall a situation where, during a negotiation, two products that complemented each other together were being offered to the customer. The customer had convinced himself that he only wanted one of the products and was not interested in paying for the second one. Going back and reviewing the original interests showed that their main goal was to speed up their production, and even though one product would help, using both would work better. Some questioning revealed that the customer was worried that his people would not be able to learn to use the second product effectively so we emphasized the simple training procedures that were available to help with that. By going back to the beginning and concentrating on the original interests and goals, we were able to break the "logjam" around that one product and resolve the negotiation successfully for both parties.

Be sensitive in dealing with the people part of the negotiation. Negotiations usually work out better when you can keep the issues separate from the people and their personalities. However, sometimes people's feelings are more important than their interests, so be careful to respect those feelings in your discussions going forward. A friendly manner without getting personal should go a long way toward a good result. Here again, good customer relationships are very important; it's much easier to negotiate with a friend than with a stranger, as there is more respect and trust. And remember to take care that your good relationships do not deteriorate during difficult negotiations. The future is often much more important than one specific situation.

If possible, be flexible — even if you don't have much room for movement. Try not to take hard and fast positions as these may cause problems if you are seen to be intractable. That means you don't want to start at your last ditch position as you will have no room for movement. Generally it is best in any negotiation to let the other part present their position or demands first. That gives you something to work with and you can get a feel for what you can do. You may have heard the old expression that says, "He who speaks first loses." That's often the case in negotiations. Silence is golden. Have a reason for speaking, or don't talk. Often typical sales personalities have a difficult time with silence. They feel they must keep selling, even in negotiations. This can lead to a "give away the store" situation, because usually the talker continues to concede when they get no response from the listener. If the other side is non-responsive to your offers, use questions and silence. Give them time to consider and to respond to what you have said.

Think win-win when going for solutions. Since many sales are ongoing, if you or the customer ends up with a bad result, it can create major problems in future dealings. For continuing business to occur, there usually has to be at least some win on both sides. For example, when negotiating a price where you are faced with inexpensive imported foreign competition often subsidized by the foreign government, you can outline the situation that will occur if the price is so low that, in the long term, your company and other domestic competitors can't make enough profit to stay in business. Since most customers do not want to rely only on foreign sources, this argument may help you get or keep the premium you want for your product or service. How much of a premium is, of course, open to negotiation, based on all the other variables that are present. It can be done, but selling intangible hypothetical situations can be a real challenge to your abilities, and you may only be able to get or keep a portion of the business. The customer sometimes has a strong position in this kind of negotiation and it can be difficult to get much of a win.

Sometimes your own position is so strong that you might need to be careful that the customer ends up with some kind of win. This could occur when you have the only product or service that will work, or the market is in short supply and you are allocating product among many customers, or some similar situation. Leaving customers with no win will generally end up with their feeling you have taken advantage of them due to your strength. Customers typically have long memories, and when the market turns, as it always does, your sales may be hurt. I have seen suppliers treat customers so badly during shortages that when supply opened up again, they lost all their business with those customers. Suppliers who were sensitive to the relationships, and allowed customers some win in the difficult situations, usually came out better when the customer was back in the driver's seat, which, in sales, is most of the time.

Some small win for the customer in a situation like this may require your freeing up a little product for them even though it may not be all they want. It may be extending credit terms temporarily to help them through a hard time because they cannot produce what they would like. You'll have to decide what options to consider, but anything you can do in these situations will help you when timing gives the customer more control.

You are likely to experience a situation where both you and the customer feel that when one of you wins, the other one loses. This may be the case, but because negotiations are not always a "zero sum game," often both parties can win. Be creative and work to find solutions that make the pie bigger so that both sides can win together; this type of thinking helps cement strong customer relationships and more opportunities for additional business.

One time we faced a situation where we were working to obtain all of a customer's business, but they were worried about supply and pricing if they were served by only one supplier. Fear of the unknown or possible bad results can sometimes make negotiations hard to resolve. We agreed to handle supply by putting a meter with a remote monitor in their tank and committing to make sure they always had sufficient product. We tied the price to a market index so they felt comfortable they were getting an excellent competitive price. As a result of this arrangement, the customer no longer needed someone to check the tank and their purchasing department didn't have to worry about pricing. In addition, now that we were the only supplier involved, we were solely responsible for problems if they occurred. Since we were testing outgoing shipments for quality, they could eliminate the redundant testing of incoming shipments from different suppliers. This program minimized labor and testing on their part, saving them significant money. We were able to schedule the shipments at our convenience and, at the same time, to make sure that they did not run out. It was a true win-win result; the pie got bigger.

No matter how good you are at negotiations, at some point reality will be against you. The customer's position may be so strong that it will seem as if you do not have even a small win available. In those cases, be sure to understand your options. What is the best alternative available if the deal doesn't happen or you do not reach agreement? This is commonly known as the BATNA, which stands for the Best Alternative To Negotiated Agreement. This analysis may reveal that you need to accept a bad deal since it still may be better than nothing at all. Or you may find that no deal or no agreement is better than a bad one. Understanding the alternatives will help you make the best decision in each case, even if it turns out that walking away is best. If you do end up walking away from a result you cannot accept, especially if you already have a good relationship otherwise, it can be a good idea to make sure the client or customer understands your reason for doing so. Maybe you can't make a profit, or maybe what they want is something that doesn't fit your business model, or perhaps you don't physically have the necessary personnel available. It can be any number of things. Offering an explanation will help the customer understand and perhaps empathize with your position. Even if you didn't reach agreement, explaining your position can allow the negotiation to end on a neutral or positive note where friendships are not ended and bridges are not burned. That will leave the door open for other possibilities in the future, which should be one of the objectives of even a bad negotiation.

Learn from all your negotiations. What was involved in achieving the result? Were you happy with the result? If not, why not? Was the result primarily a problem with the parameters, or was your performance a factor? What could you have done better? Since there is normally a wide spectrum of possible outcomes, and you won't always get a good result, were there areas in which you could have done more to achieve a better result? Analyzing each negotiation will help you improve.

One final note; it may help you to sit down with the procurement people in your company and ask them what they look for when negotiating with salespeople who call on them. What are their negotiation tactics and strategy? Or, take a negotiation class that is specific to procurement professionals. Learn to think like your customers think. And prepare, prepare, and prepare some more. The more prepared you are for a negotiation, the more likely you are to achieve a better outcome.

I always felt that negotiating was one of the most interesting and exciting parts of selling. You can feel the adrenaline flowing during the process, and when things start coming together you will achieve a great feeling of satisfaction. The more capable a negotiator you become, the more frequently you will achieve this satisfaction. If you are careful to maintain good customer relationships, even through difficult negotiations, that will contribute even more to your ultimate success.

★★★★★
POINTS

- ★ Establish agreement on the facts
- ★ Restate to show you understand the other side's position
- ★ Be alert for the "people part" of the negotiations
- ★ Often, silence is golden
- ★ Listen, listen, listen… before speaking
- ★ Identify shared interests
- ★ Try to look at the issues from the same side
- ★ Try for agreement on the broad goals
- ★ Work for win-win as much as possible
- ★ If there is no "win" for you, evaluate your "BATNA" and be prepared to walk away
- ★ Try to maintain the relationship
- ★ Learn to improve from all your negotiations, both good and bad
- ★ Practice—you will get better
- ★ Consider learning negotiating strategy and tactics from the procurement side as well

CHAPTER 15: PROBLEMS
Are These Really Opportunities in Disguise?

Unfortunately, everyone sooner or later encounters a situation where you or your company blunders, a misunderstanding occurs, or for some other reason you have a highly dissatisfied customer. How you handle a mistake, problem, or complaint can often make or break your relationship with the customer. If you can work through the troublesome issue as soon as possible showing your concern, you will retain more goodwill with the customer than if you ignore the situation. In fact, if you deal with the situation correctly, then a blunder on the part of you or your company may end up strengthening, rather than weakening your relationship.

Let me tell you about a simple situation that happened to me. While living in Charlotte, North Carolina, I once took a favorite shirt to a local dry cleaner. Unfortunately, when I went to pick it up, I noticed that they had somehow gotten a huge stain on the front of it and it was no longer wearable. Since I liked the shirt, I was quite irritated and pointed out the problem to the employee behind the counter. She asked me politely what I had paid for the shirt. I told her I could not remember but gave her what I thought was a close approximation. Without missing a beat, she reached into the cash register drawer and gave me the money saying, "I'm sorry for what happened. We cannot fix the shirt, but hopefully this will help you replace it." She may not have considered herself a salesperson, but she certainly stepped into the role that day. I'm sure you can guess where I had all my dry cleaning done the remainder of the time I lived in Charlotte. You will also note the fact that almost every job can benefit from good salesmanship.

Salespeople can often do the same kind of things. After you have been with your company for a while, you will generally know the limits of what you can do to solve many problems by yourself. Perhaps you can approve up to a certain monetary level without requiring management to "sign off" on it. If so, you can take some approvals into your own hands. Own the account and do what is needed when it is needed without having to go back and ask for permission unless necessary. You should look at your territory as your own little company. What happens there directly affects your business. It is up to you to make it profitable. So, if you can resolve the issue yourself, do it. If it takes more than that, or perhaps you already see that you can't solve the problem in the manner the customer wants, explain to them that you need to consult with people inside your company, that you will see what you can do, and will get back to them quickly. Then make certain you follow up right away. Don't let problems sit around and stagnate. They won't go away; they will only get worse. Doing all the things we discussed in Chapter 11, on selling internally, will increase your ability to engage the willing help of people in your own company.

Be sure to give a problem the attention it deserves. Not much irritates a person more than the feeling they are not being taken seriously. I once received an unexpected phone call from the vice president of one of my largest accounts, asking when I would be in their area for my next visit. My contact with this individual before this point had been minimal, so the fact that he called me was very unusual. To determine the best course of action, I asked for details of what was needed. He told me that he felt they had been badly treated in a recent allocation of product, and thought they deserved much better. The situation seemed critical to them. He believed they were being ignored and wanted to talk with me about it. It was obvious he was quite upset. It was going to be a few weeks before I was next scheduled to see them, so I decided to interrupt my sector call plan (see Chapter 2) and visit him right away. I told him I would see what I could do and would call him back immediately. When I was able to make plane reservations that day, I called him to see if he would have dinner that evening and then we could meet to go over the issues the next morning. Because our relationship with this large company to this point had always been excellent, he agreed to do that. Since, as I mentioned, I did not know this gentleman well, we spent the dinner not discussing business but getting better acquainted. I arrived the next morning for the meeting to discuss his concerns, and he spent considerable time and energy getting several complaints off his chest. He thought a once excellent relationship was going bad and that the people at our company were not attentive to their needs any longer. He used the major specific current allocation problem as an example and went on from there. For about an hour I just listened to everything he had to say. When he was through, I told him that even though allocation plans were developed by our product management people, I felt — as his salesperson — that the overall responsibility was mine. I promised to check out the facts and the parameters and respond as soon as I could get the information. I then spent some time pointing out the many positives that I believed were still present in the relationship between the two companies and the strong history we had together. I told him I might not be able to solve this specific problem, because product was in very tight supply, but I would make sure they were getting their fair share. It was a long and exhausting discussion. No solution was readily apparent, but we left the issue as one we would work on together.

As I was getting up to leave, the vice president stopped me and said, "Lee, I have to give you credit. We are unhappy and angry. You know that. As a result of what we thought was happening, we were planning to cut back our business with your company. You responded very quickly. You didn't say you could solve the problem, but you listened patiently, and I believe you will do your best to help us. No matter what happens in the future between us and our companies, I only hope that if any of our salespeople were faced with a situation like this, they would handle themselves as well as you have."

Imagine my feelings. I appreciated his compliment, of course, but the basic lesson is that I had given them enough respect to change my schedule, and then was careful to listen, listen, and listen. The meeting ended on a very friendly note, which gave us the time to work on the problems. We didn't do everything they wanted, but we were able to make some changes. The quick response, and giving them the attention they deserved, went a long way toward turning that situation around. And, as it turned out, we didn't lose any business.

Be creative in responding to problem situations. One salesperson found himself in the position of having to make a call on a large customer after his company had just made a major mistake. He knew it was going to be a very difficult call, so he decided on the very unusual action of going to a costume supplier and renting a suit of armor. He walked into the purchasing agent's office with his arms sticking out to the sides and metal clanking everywhere. He dropped the visor and said, "I know we really screwed up and there's nothing I can do at this point to reverse the past and change what happened, so I'm here to take my medicine ... give me your best shot and then we'll try to fix it."

The customer cracked up. He was still upset, but the ice was broken and the atmosphere became conducive to alleviating the problem. A little extreme, but very creative! And it worked in that case.

Be creative in seeking solutions. Look for some kind of win-win way to solve a problem, if possible. If something happened where the customer is demanding a cash settlement and you were really at fault, perhaps you can offer to give him the equivalent amount in product. That way the customer gets equal value but your company only suffers the cost of the product, and continues to supply them. This gives you time to repair the damage to the relationship. That can be a true win-win in a bad situation. If the customer is looking for reimbursement for the value of his product that was ruined by something your company did, try to get them to agree to their "out-of-pocket costs" only. Usually, their unrealized profit can be removed from the settlement. Maybe you can be creative with credit terms to solve a problem. Perhaps you can offer some other perks instead of cash. I have seen many interesting and creative solutions to both very small and very large problems that were accepted by customers.

As you seek to solve problems, it's always good to dig a little to ensure that what your customers are saying is really what they mean, and that it represents the "whole problem." Ask a question like, "Along with this, is there anything else we need to look at that you are concerned about?" This may unearth another significant part of the problem or a totally new issue.

Occasionally, problems don't have win-win solutions, but you will be surprised at how many *do*. It is not easy to search for ways that both you and the customer can benefit as problems get worked out, but it's certainly worth doing. Sometimes problems don't seem to have a positive side, but often they really are opportunities. I have seen numerous occasions where problems handled quickly and efficiently have resulted in increased business. After a customer understands that you will not run away from a problem, or offer an endless string of excuses, a higher level of trust is created, and they are more likely to be open with you. That ultimately helps the relationship, and you will be more likely to keep — and even grow — your business.

★ ★ ★ ★ ★
POINTS

- ★ When facing problems, have an idea of what you can do and resolve them yourself if you can
- ★ Start the problem-solving process quickly and follow up
- ★ Take the customer seriously
- ★ First: listen, listen, listen
- ★ Search for win-win solutions
- ★ Be creative
- ★ Make sure you are addressing the underlying concerns
- ★ Problems really can be opportunities if handled properly

CHAPTER 16: ENTERTAINMENT
Is It Important?

Can entertainment help with sales? The short answer is, "It depends." The longer answer is that the decision should be based on your company's guidelines, the value of the customer, the customer's views, and what you are trying to achieve. For many companies, entertaining customers is not part of their sales effort. Sometimes it's the customers who won't allow their people to participate. However, if your company's selling approach encourages appropriate entertainment, it can be very effective in furthering your customer relationships.

There is not much benefit in entertaining a customer with little potential, or one where relationships with the purchasing department are discouraged. Determining the potential should have been accomplished following the steps outlined in "Getting Organized," Chapter 2. For customers who actively discourage relationships with their buyers, entertainment is usually not a winning path. I know of one very large company which changes their buyers every six months, just so there will be no relationships with the salespeople. For them, price is the primary objective. Since most buying decisions they make come down to price, they don't want relationships influencing purchasing decisions at all. Obviously, in situations like that, entertainment is of no value.

For customers with larger potential where entertainment would help the relationships and is appropriate, let's assume your company allows and supports the use of customer entertainment as part of your sales arsenal. It is a powerful sales tool if used properly. It is best if you inherit a good relationship from the former salesperson, because that gives you a good start, but even if that's not the case, you can begin on the right path for what you want to accomplish.

First, you need to understand that effective entertainment is not used to "buy the business." There are some customers who may pressure you for "gifts" or exorbitant entertainment, but you should realize that responding to that pressure is a losing game. In the long run, if you are trying to "buy the business" with entertainment or gifts, you will lose the respect of the customer and/or his or her supervisor, and probably your management as well. It's a no-win situation, because there is usually a competitor who is willing to spend more.

Although it is not entertainment per se, there are situations where small gifts may be appropriate to your selling effort. The key word is "small." One salesperson used to take a few dozen doughnuts every time he visited one of his major customers and gave them to the plant employees who used his products in manufacturing. Another took her clients a box of chocolates with her company's logo on them at holiday occasions. These kinds of small gifts are usually considered tokens of thanks; if they are looked at as more than that, you have not accomplished your purpose and, ultimately, may hurt your sales effort.

Entertainment should be used as a tool leading to better and deeper relationships. Occasions, such as lunch, dinner, concerts, golf outings, or other events, are opportunities to get to know the individuals that make the buying decisions. People buy from people, not just from companies. The better your customer or prospect knows you, and you them, the more they will respect you, trust you, like you, and want to work with you—not because you entertained them but because they will have come to know the kind of person you are and what you represent. All of this helps to build the kind of relationship where you and the customer can work together more effectively, develop a higher level of trust, and accomplish more win-win situations.

Some of the general principles for entertainment are:

1. **Include at least a light business discussion — after all, you are still selling.**
2. **Only entertain those customers and prospects where there is potential or current value.**
3. **The event or process should be enjoyable for everyone.**
4. **It should promote friendship and trust, which means you must be present. For example, don't just give tickets away if you don't plan to attend as well.**
5. **Be aware of your limits and budget; lavish is not always best.**
6. **If you are selling abroad as well as in the United States, be aware of cultural differences among people.**

It is also important for the business relationship that any entertainment is in harmony with the customer's personal values and style, and with your own. If you are uncomfortable with certain types of entertainment or other awkward business situations, take the lead and make alternate suggestions before being put in a difficult position. For example, if you feel certain types of entertainment are inappropriate, suggest something in advance like a sporting event, or perhaps a family-oriented event, which might include spouses and maybe even children. In some cases, this strategy gets things started in the direction you want and can reduce the potential for problems associated with other types of entertainment.

It may occur that an account is being transferred to you from another salesperson, and entertainment is involved as part of the transfer. If your style is different from the previous salesperson's style, make sure to discuss it with him or her — before the customer is involved — so that the subsequent entertainment works within your own style. If something is suggested that you feel doesn't fit you or reflect what you'd like the customer to think about you, suggest another idea for something that does. Don't be dogmatic or judgmental, just offer alternatives. You want and need to familiarize the customer with what you are like. You do not have to perpetuate an uncomfortable entertainment relationship just because you inherited it from a salesperson with values different from yours. On *rare* occasions you will encounter a proposed activity where friendship with the client and respect from the client are mutually exclusive and you will need to choose. If this happens, my advice is to choose respect.

Here are some ways to avoid problematic situations:

1. **Ask your clients about their families and talk about your family.**
2. **Steer conversations away from questionable topics.**
3. **Search for common values and interests, and focus on them.**
4. **Make the customer aware of your values before potential problem situations come up. You don't have to be blunt about it, just be willing to "reveal" things about yourself early in the relationship that let them know the kind of person you are. People are not likely to criticize your values and concerns as long as you don't try to push them on others.**
5. **If the relationship is built on respect, even if their values are different from yours, the customer will usually not suggest doing anything that will make you uncomfortable. However, if they do, and you have to choose between their respect and their friendship, choose respect.**
6. **Don't take yourself too seriously — be tolerant.**
7. **Take the lead in potentially awkward situations, and state your preference first.**
8. **Be creative — sometimes unusual entertainment opportunities are best.**
9. **Remember that, generally, others want you to like and respect them as much as you want to be liked and respected.**

Try to provide memorable entertainment opportunities rather than lavish ones. Don't be afraid to be creative. Take pictures during the event and give them to the customer afterwards. This creates memories for the customer. Get them mentally "far away from the office." In situations which fit your objectives, entertain your customers with their families. On one occasion, as a salesperson in the Chicago area, I planned a charter fishing trip on Lake Michigan well in advance. We usually had no problem lining up customers — because we always had success catching very large king salmon and lake trout — but on this occasion, several customers dropped out at the last minute for a variety of reasons. Unfortunately, we could not cancel the charter at that late date, and the down payment was already invested. I did not want to invite other customers at that point, because they would realize they were second choices. After thinking about an alternate idea and discussing the situation with my sales manager, who was scheduled to go along, I called up the one large prospect that hadn't canceled and suggested he bring his son along. When he agreed, since my son was around the same age (about twelve), he was included as well.

You can imagine the excitement as these youngsters hooked into those monster salmon. It was an outing to remember. At the time, my company wasn't doing very much business with this prospect, and it had been hard to really get to know this purchasing manager. Our fishing trip broke the ice and, a month or so later, my family was invited by the customer to a family picnic in his community. Those two family occasions built trust and respect between the two of us, and our business grew along with it. In hindsight, the power of entertainment like this seems obvious. And, as it turned out, my sales manager thought the fishing trip that included the kids was a brilliant idea when, in fact, I just made the best of a problem situation and it worked.

Try different things. Excellent entertainment should be more than lunches, dinners, and predictable events — and it doesn't have to be expensive. I had customers who played tennis, so we put together tennis outings for almost no cost. Another customer was a hiker, so we tried that together once (he left me in the dust, but we had a good time). And be careful that you don't gravitate to only one type of entertainment. I knew one salesperson that would rather play golf than eat.

He had several customers who enjoyed golf, so golf outings became a regular form of entertainment for him. Unfortunately, it was the only thing he did, so those customers who were not golfers were neglected. Creative entertainment can fit many circumstances. For example, if your client is a golfer and you don't have the time for an entire 18-hole round, you might offer them a golf lesson after lunch at the club or at a driving range. Most golfers would find that an offer hard to refuse. It takes nowhere near as long and you still get face time with your customer. Sales entertainment requires that you be willing to go along with the interests of others. Some of those might not be first on your list, but they will further your relationships.

If you are not married, you won't have a problem with entertainment occasions where spouses are not typically included. However, in family-oriented situations, you may want to bring a guest so everyone will feel more comfortable. One of our salespeople always brought a date to dinners where the customer's spouse was included.

During the process of entertaining customers at dinner (or even at lunches, occasionally), and at trade shows or similar occasions, you will likely be exposed to alcohol. Whether you choose to drink or not is a personal decision. Most customers will respect your choice, but occasionally you will run into one who wants you to drink with them. Fortunately, that is not as prevalent as when there really were "three martini lunches," but sometimes it can still be an issue. Here are a few suggestions to handle this situation. If you do not drink, just quietly order a soft drink or club soda. Your client or customer will get the picture. You can be clear but be careful not to appear judgmental of others.

If you drink but prefer not to on some occasions you can either decline or try some other technique. I used to "beg off" by saying I was taking medication when I was with a hard-drinking customer. One salesperson I knew ordered a gin and tonic for his first drink and later, on his way to the restroom, quietly asked the waiter to leave the gin out of subsequent rounds, without saying anything about what he was doing. However, if you do choose to join them in a drink, know your limits. Do not, under any circumstances, have too many drinks with either your customers or your management. I have seen sales careers go down the drain because the salesperson did not know when enough was enough. Also be aware of the problems associated with drinking and driving. It is better to call a cab if someone in your group is not available to be the "designated driver."

Understand the company policy in regard to the relationship of what you should be spending based on the value of the customer. Don't spend big dollars on small customers. Don't spend an inordinate amount on some chosen clients just because they have become friends.

Learn a little about wines so that, when you are dining with a customer, you can order the wine yourself—not the least expensive, or the most expensive, but something in the middle that fits the occasion. Don't trust the wait staff or the customer. I was present when one of our salespeople offered to let the customer order the wine, not realizing he was a wine connoisseur. The salesperson ended up with a bill where the wine cost twice as much as the dinner. I also recall an occasion when we were celebrating a very good year with about six of our customer's management and four of our top people at an elegant restaurant. After dinner, the waiter offered glasses of port that had been aged since before World War II. Fortunately, our customers were intelligent enough to defer, and we were as well. It turned out those glasses of port were priced at about $125 each — my sales budget certainly couldn't have stood that.

Here's another important point. Carry enough cash to cover the unexpected. If you are going to a new restaurant for dinner, you should check ahead of time to see if they take credit cards. Even some upscale eateries only take cash and, if you don't have it, a problem may develop. A colleague told me about an occasion that occurred shortly after being assigned to his first sales territory. After dinner with several customers, he found the restaurant would not accept credit cards. During a discreet discussion with the manager, he talked them into taking one of his predecessor's calling cards with the name scratched out (he hadn't gotten his cards yet) and his name inserted and they agreed to bill him. Apparently, that fellow already knew how to sell — and it also helped that he was representing a major company with a household name — but you may not be that lucky.

I once took a customer to lunch at a new place he suggested, only to find when I checked that I did not have enough cash to cover the bill, and they did not take credit cards. I'd known the customer for some time, so he agreed to loan me some money to cover the bill. Fortunately, we were able to put together what money I had and enough of his cash to pay the bill. I sent him a check in the mail as soon as I got home. It all worked out, but it was quite an embarrassing experience, and one I never repeated. From that point on, I always checked my cash reserves before heading out to lunch with a customer.

It seems obvious, but with any major entertainment, make sure all your people have the appropriate information about the guests who will be attending. This includes keeping everyone's spouses informed as well, if they will be joining you. At one major dinner, the spouse of one of our salespeople ended up sitting next to the CEO of a major customer. His office was the whole top floor of a building his company owned in downtown Chicago, and he lived nearby in an apartment over Bloomingdale's. In the course of the conversation, not realizing his stature in the business world, our salesperson's spouse asked him if he walked to work or took the bus. He was gracious and just smiled and said his company provided security and sent a car for him every day. Another time, a customer was asked which airline he took to the meeting when he had come in on their company's corporate jet. Important people often like to be treated as such. These are small things to be sure, but it's always good for everyone to be informed about the people in attendance so little blunders do not occur.

Entertaining can be fun, and it's certainly a great way to develop excellent business relationships. If it's appropriate to your business, do a little entertaining, get to know your customers better, and let them learn more about you. Again, remember, people buy from people they know, they like, and they trust. Be one of those people.

★ ★ ★ ★ ★
POINTS

★ The entertainment time and expense should be appropriate to the value of the account — you decide where your entertainment budget dollars are best spent
★ Use entertainment to get to know customers better, not to "buy business"
★ Better relationships build friendships, respect, and trust
★ Don't "inherit and perpetuate" problematic entertainment situations — decide what you think is right and initiate your own style
★ Set the tone for the type of entertainment where both you and the customer are comfortable
★ If you can't have both, go for respect over friendship; it's better not to compromise your value system
★ Be creative, make entertainment memorable
★ Alcohol can cause big problems; plan how you will deal with it and know your limits
★ Be prepared for places that do not take credit cards
★ Make sure everyone involved is informed of all important details in advance
★ Always remember, people buy from people

CHAPTER 18: DEALING WITH EXPENSES
Keep Track and Keep Your Sanity!

Having reviewed hundreds of expense statements over the years, I have noticed that handling expenses can be difficult for many salespeople. Sometimes the problem is dealing with the paperwork and details; sometimes it is controlling the spending. Salespeople are not necessarily detail-oriented by nature, but if you are not careful, all sorts of things can start falling through the cracks.

Good salespeople can lose significant money in lack of reimbursement if they mishandle their expenses or fail to report sales expenses properly. If not corrected, their jobs may be at risk. I'm not talking about the cheaters, the few that try to falsify their expense statements for personal gain — which is theft. I'm talking about typical salespeople who are a lot more excited by other parts of the job and sometimes let expenses, and expense reporting, slide. Some salespeople's expense statements are routinely late. They may also contain numerous errors — improper documentation, lost receipts, inadequate justifications — and are often simply incomplete. This sloppy handling of funds can become a disaster. Having a little discipline and a system that works for you is extremely important. Here are a few approaches that may help.

It's best to keep a separate bank account used only for business expenses. Start with enough money in it to handle the cycle of reimbursement. Using a separate credit card for business expenses will help you retain the receipts as a reminder for you, and to satisfy the IRS requirements. After lunches or dinners, when I was given the credit card receipt from the wait staff, it helped me to quickly write on the back of it the names and titles, if necessary, of the people who were present. (This was especially important if anyone attended that I had not met previously.) This simple habit ensured that I would remember their names and how to spell them when filling out the expense statement later. Receipts often need to be included with the expense statement, so it is good to have a regular routine or place to keep track of them. If you don't get a receipt for something, where one does not need to be submitted, you can write a short reminder and handle that the same way, so you don't forget the expense and details. Also, it is very important to pay the credit card bill in full as soon as it comes. I knew one salesperson that got so far behind with payments that he had to use reimbursement for current expenses to pay the credit card bill for past expenses. As you would expect, it caught up with him. When he was asked to resign for a totally different reason, he still owed a considerable sum to a major credit card company.

Don't let expenses mount up before getting them in the system for reimbursement. Expense reports should always be done by the end of the week; do not let them run into the next week. There may be occasions, such as a long business trip, where you might wait until you get back to submit the expenses, but at least keep up with them weekly as you go along. Remember, unless you are using a company credit card where the company is billed directly, it is your money and you want it back! Every salesperson typically carries a device of some sort for recording data, and readily-available expense reporting software makes it easy to input the information on a daily basis. These applications can also print completed expense reports in many types of formats, depending on your needs and your company's requirements.

If your company does not have a system for you to submit expenses, or if you are an independent salesperson who is responsible for your own, you might want to work with a weekly expense sheet that looks something like the one shown on the next page.

It's easy to set up a spreadsheet like this, where all you have to do is enter the numbers and it's added up automatically for you. You can add or remove headings for the expense categories that you need to report. If any of the expenses require more detail, you should use the comment section at the bottom with the date, category, and explanation.

IRS regulations require specific information about the business purpose and attendees of a meeting where entertainment is involved. Be sure to comply with these rules, especially if yours is a small

EXPENSE RECORD: WEEK OF 3/04/2014
BOB LAYMEX | 101 GROVE STREET | KANSAS CITY, MO

Date	Airfare*	Misc*	Parking and Tolls	Car Rental	Hotel	Food	Entertainment	Total Expenses	Activity
3/04/2014									
3/05/2014	$763.00	$28.00	$3.25		$126.00	27.55	30.33	$978.13	Travel to Kansas City
3/06/2014			$16.30		$126.00	$29.32	$55.35	$226.97	Calls in Kansas City
3/07/2014			$15.50	$68.42	$111.00	$7.80	$235.37	$438.09	Calls in Omaha
3/08/2014		$28.00		$78.33	$113.00	$24.94	$38.40	$282.67	Wichita Calls / Travel Home
3/09/2014		$55.28						$55.28	Office Day
3/10/2014									
Totals	$763.00	$111.28	$35.05	$146.75	$476.00	$89.61	$359.45	1981.14	

Comments:

3/05/2014	Misc.	Cab to airport
3/08/2014	Misc.	Cab home from airport
3/09/2014	Misc.	Purchase of shredder for confidential business documents
		* Requires Explanation

business. The IRS can come down hard on those who provide inadequate documentation of entertainment and travel expenses. They also require a reason for non-business personnel, such as spouses, to be present. If it's a dinner, for example, when a customer's spouse would be present, a statement like "Mrs. Johnson normally accompanies her husband on these occasions" is usually sufficient. However, I am not an expert on IRS regulations, which change from year to year, so if your company does not have guidelines to follow, I strongly recommend that you familiarize yourself with the current IRS rules about business and entertainment expenses. These should guide you when reporting your expenses, since most companies base their own rules on these criteria. See IRS Publication 535 Business Expenses and IRS Form 2106 Employee Business Expenses.

Although you can include all the appropriate required information on the bottom under the "Comments" section of the Expense Record for items that require a longer explanation, it may be better to use an attachment that may look like this:

ADDITIONAL EXPENSE EXPLANATIONS
WEEK OF MARCH 4, 2014

Entertainment Expenses:

3/05/14 – $30.33

Lunch with John Hans and Derek Barnes of EX Space. Derek and I discussed contacts in the sporting goods industry where we might be able to help expand his sales of our new line of camping equipment.

3/06/14 – $55.35

Lunch with Frank Katz and Dick Carrier of Advanced Mineralogists. We reviewed their evaluation of the hiking line and related accessories.

3/7/14 - $44.22

Lunch with Mary Elder and John Schmidt of NLG Ind. We looked at their needs for additional equipment for the upcoming two quarters.

3/07/14 – $191.15

Dinner with Paul Buchold of Spanner Ind. We discussed the appropriate tools for repairing the Challenger equipment line. Mrs. Buchold normally accompanies her husband on these occasions.

3/8/14 - $38.40

Lunch with Bob Bircher of On Tap. We reviewed the CO_2 equipment he would need to produce their new beverage.

Of course, you can use as many lines as needed to cover the situation for each occasion.

Don't be tempted to "pad" your expenses or try to slide a few things through the system. I can tell you from experience in reviewing expense statements that it won't work for long. Most sales managers have seen it all before. A few anomalies will pop up and a little digging will cause the whole situation to unravel. I remember a salesperson who started making a habit of taking out his girlfriend and using the receipts as documentation for fictional customer entertainment, planning to get reimbursement for those personal occasions. Unfortunately for him, he called with his sales manager on a customer who, according to the salesperson's expense statement, had supposedly been to dinner with him recently. The manager innocently asked about the restaurant, commenting that he had heard it was very good. It was obvious the customer had never been there. The whole scheme came out in the open and the salesperson was fired. One of our salespeople filled up his "company car" with 16 gallons of gas. Unfortunately the real company car's fuel tank only held 12 gallons when empty. Not a major cost to the company, but also not a good representation of the salesperson's integrity.

In our company the salespeople had credit cards issued by the company for things like air travel, but the salespeople were responsible for paying the bill, and the company would reimburse them for the expenses as they were submitted. This arrangement was beneficial for the salespeople, as we usually received the reimbursement before the credit card bills were due. One salesperson tried to game the system by buying airline tickets on his credit card, and then used his frequent flyer miles for the travel. After the trip, he turned the unused tickets back in to the airline for reimbursement to his credit card bill, planning to keep the money. He didn't realize that, since it was a company-sponsored credit card, they also got a copy of the bills and credits. The internal auditors noticed that he was getting money back for the purchased tickets he turned in (and had not used), but was not reimbursing the company for the ticket refunds from the airlines. He did a lot of flying, so by the time all that caught up with him he was in debt to the company for over $6,000, had committed fraud in the process, and his great sales job went down the drain. Just be honest, charge back what you spend on company business and, assuming you are spending the money in your budget wisely, you will be in good shape.

If you are an independent business person without a company reporting expense system, even if your record keeping may not need to be as detailed as described here, you should at least keep track of mileage and vehicle expenses and other important business related costs to obtain the appropriate tax deductions. Although keeping track of expenses may not be a very exciting or enjoyable part of the sales job, remember it is extremely important. It has the attention of management (and the IRS), and therefore needs to be done properly. Stay on top of it, submit the information promptly and accurately, and everything will be fine.

★ ★ ★ ★ ★

POINTS

★ Expense reporting is important — keep it prompt and accurate
★ Open or keep a separate bank account
★ Develop a simple system for keeping up with the receipts and important information so you will not forget
★ Don't be tempted to "cheat" — it will always catch up with you over time

CHAPTER 18: KEEP IT GOING
Riding the Crest of the Wave

After you have mastered the basics of selling, it is time to "step things up a notch." When you have developed strong business relationships and are beginning to see success, it is important to stay on track. Be sure to continue to do what has been successful. Don't neglect established customers. Continue to make calls in person regularly, and use phone calls or email to stay in touch during the interim.

At this point, if you haven't begun already, it is a good idea to start "calling in depth." This means you should start developing contacts with other appropriate people at the customer's business who can affect your success and begin meeting with them as well. This can be tricky since your primary contact may feel threatened, but it's still very important to do, especially with your larger accounts. We have touched on this concept in other parts of the book, and offered several ideas on how to accomplish meeting others at the account. Sometimes it happens normally in the course of business when you meet with other purchasing people, technical people, administration people or others. Sometimes you have to engineer the opportunities by involving your management or other people in your company to facilitate meeting with other contacts. It's very important to "call in depth," because many excellent customer relationships have disappeared when the one and only contact the salesperson knew was replaced or moved on.

We talked about the importance of internal selling in Chapter 11, and your management should certainly be part of this equation. As business grows, your management can help you open the door to seeing your customer's higher management (also see Chapter 12). With care, you can use calls with management to facilitate in-depth calls without offending your primary contact. A side benefit of developing deeper relationships between your management team and the customer's management is that you will find it easier to sell *internally* — to your own management — on following a course of action you want to implement for that customer. It is much harder for management to deny your requests when they know the customer contacts personally.

It's important to be an advocate for your customers inside your company. Your customers are looking for you to "represent" them to your company, just as you are representing your company to *them*. It is a fine line to walk, but one of the highest compliments you can get is when your customers indicate that they do not look at you as a supplier, but as an extension of their own companies. You should also be using the rest of your team. When appropriate, schedule opportunities for others at your company to meet additional people at the customers' companies to help you sell. If cost is an issue, think about using an internet interface. When your technical people, engineers, or other non-sales colleagues can meet with their counterparts at your customers' places of business, great things can happen. If you listen carefully to their discussions with the customer, you can use that same information when calling on smaller customers where bringing the other people in does not make sense from a cost standpoint. Plus, your customers will respect your developed technical expertise as well. I often took our engineering and technical people to see the larger customers and listened carefully to what they said. Later, my smaller customers heard the same information from me. It works.

You will find that even if you happen to be very knowledgeable on a product or service you are selling, the customer may still request to hear it from the "experts" inside the company. Before I started selling, I worked in a development and technical service laboratory. As it turned out later, I inherited an account in my first territory that was interested in a new product I had developed while in the laboratory. After waxing enthusiastic about the benefits of this product, I was crushed when the customer asked me to check with the lab people to confirm some of the information I had presented. Even though I knew this particular product inside and out, I checked with the laboratory to see if there was anything new. Nothing had changed, so I just reported back to him the comments "from the lab." Of course, if I hadn't been very familiar with that product, I might have had to learn much more from our technical people to feel comfortable answering the cus-tomer's questions. This is another situation where you might use your company's technological capabilities and use an internet interface to work with those customers.

Make sure your pricing is competitive, especially if you have all the business. This is extremely important. If a customer would give me 100% of his business, I would guarantee to keep him competitive with other customers his size in the marketplace. Trying to get a premium because he is buying his total requirement from you and is not check-ing the market is a quick way to lose this trusted business. The only way to get a reasonable premium is to have a product or service (or some combination of both) that is better than the competitor's, and to have the customer recognize that and be willing to pay for it.

Look for opportunities where your company is uniquely different and try to leverage that. Sometimes that will allow premium prices for your products or services. In our case, we offered much more tech-nical service to our customers than was available from our competi-tors. Although this was an additional cost to our company, many of our customers valued the extra service and were still willing to buy from us even on those occasions when our pricing was slightly higher. When we had to be competitive, the extra volume generated by the additional service helped cover the additional costs.

To make the value of our technical service clearer to the customers and to minimize the effects of our reluctance to be the first to lower pric-es, we developed an approach we called "competitive plus." This method ensured that our customers were aware of, and valued, all the extra ser-vice we offered. We pointed out that this type of service was available from us at competitive pricing. We communicated that if they would keep us informed when lower prices became available to them, we would meet the competitive price, and all the extra service would continue to benefit them at no extra charge. When the customers understood our position, we were very successful in earning the "second looks" that were important to us in keeping their business. Because many of our customers wanted the extras we provided, and knew our price would be equal to the best domestic price they could get elsewhere, they were willing to give us those second looks and keep their business with us. In the process, by not aggressively lowering prices, as mentioned above, we more than paid for the cost of the additional technical service.

Be familiar with the "extras" your company has that the customer wants. Many times those extras will get you second looks on pricing or a second chance at the sale. Your company might include service contracts with equipment or IT (information technology), follow-up with software applications, or on-site technical assistance. It's like a car dealer who washes your car or offers a free oil change, or has a policy to give you a loaner when you take it in for service. Are those kinds of things an edge? Of course they are — if you have them, sell them! The possibilities for leveraging opportunities are endless.

Of course your company may be much like the rest of your competitors in your industry, without anything extra to offer. This is often the case in highly competitive commodity markets. Still, this is good news for you, the salesperson, because this is your opportunity to *make* the difference. If you follow the ideas presented in this book, you will definitely stand out and, all things being equal, they will want to buy from *you*.

If you are selling for a company with products or services that the customers want, priced commensurately with their value, and that have developed a following in the marketplace, you are in a great situation. If you are willing to do the fundamental requirements to become an excellent salesperson, there is no end in sight. You will succeed.

★ ★ ★ ★ ★
POINTS

- ★ Keep doing the things that have made you successful
- ★ Draw on management and other internal people at your company when appropriate to supplement your effort
- ★ Be an advocate for your customer inside your own company
- ★ Stay competitive, use extras to get "second looks"
- ★ Be better than the others — remember people buy from people

Chapter 19: Taking Sales to the Highest Level
Achieving Excellence

So where do you go from here? That's really up to you. You will find that you can get pretty far along with just the basics, because many salespeople have not even mastered the first steps. Eventually, if you are serious about being a top-notch salesperson with a great career, you will realize that you need to add some new skills. You will have been in some difficult discussions with customers whose questions or requests you weren't ready to deal with. You will have been involved in sales situations that you were uncertain how to handle. Various complex sales circumstances are starting to pop up and you are not sure what to do.

Here are a few suggestions:

Find mentors throughout your career.

Find people in or outside your company that you respect, who understand what you are trying to do, and seek their help. If they are familiar with your sales process it may be possible to ask them to be your coach. A person in a coaching role is closer to the situation and may be able to see the picture more clearly. A coach can give you feedback, constructive criticism, and many other things you may need. Be respectful, listen, and follow their advice. If you are unwilling to do that, tactfully make them aware of why you are taking a different approach. You may lose a mentor or coach, and that may be OK, but carefully review the entire process as you go forward.

Use your own ingenuity.

I found myself spending time after calls thinking about what I should have said that I had not thought of at the time. It didn't take me long to figure out what I could have done or said that would have worked out better (it's amazing how much better you think when you are not "on the spot"). I began to practice those responses until they were second nature. It's not surprising that the same things come up again and again, so after you work out how to handle them, you are way ahead of the game. You won't get flustered, and you will be able to handle the common, but difficult, questions very easily. Many of the tough questions will be about price, or price increases, so the answers to these customer concerns ought to be at the top of your prepared response list. Practice new things or ideas on smaller customers or in less critical situations. See how they work. Learn as you go. Your responses cannot sound like canned or prepared "speeches," but should be well thought out, sincere, and appropriate to the situation. In most cases, with some preparation beforehand, you will be sensitive enough to understand what is needed and be ready to handle it.

Talk things over with your best management people.

In many cases they have dealt with these situations before and can help you in learning how to handle them. Give them a call before trying to handle a difficult problem you have not faced before. A better plan than just asking them for advice or what to do is to develop a few alternative courses of action and ask them for some feedback. This lets them know you are capable of developing possible solutions on your own. They may mention some ideas that you haven't considered or just help you fine tune one of your own. Benefit from their experience. Generally, they like being asked.

Before asking, be sure the situation is worth asking for input. By this time, you are a professional so management will be expecting you to deal with smaller issues on your own. Obviously, you will be asking for more help when you are new, but as you mature in sales you will encounter fewer and fewer situations you cannot handle yourself.

Continue to read and study.

As with any profession, the more you learn about selling, the better prepared you will be. Read books about listening, questioning, and closing. Learn the techniques of the pros in your field. Read books about people skills and about persistence and perseverance and overcoming objections and obstacles. Read material on performance management. Sharpen your tools. Many sales books will not fit your field, or perhaps they will be unsuited to your personality or method of selling. Many will be right on target. Take outside sales seminars if appropriate. Expose yourself to lots of new ideas and pick the ones that work for you.

Work more on your strengths than your weaknesses.

This is a good idea unless the weak areas are critical to your success. Many salespeople are continually admonished by their management to work hard on deficient administrative skills, or writing call reports, or other similar "areas for improvement" where many typical salespeople have problems. Although a certain level of competence in all skill areas is necessary, I suggest you spend much more time and effort on maximizing your strengths, which hopefully include the critical ones like people skills, call preparation, follow-up, negotiation, and the other important strengths you need when dealing directly with the customers.

Some salespeople feel that if they are producing great sales results, neglecting other things will be overlooked. However, it is not an option to send in expense reports several weeks late, or to neglect to submit call reports or other paperwork. Although everyone doesn't see it this way, in my experience it is much more productive to get these less important areas to the minimum acceptable level and then work on raising them later after you are very accomplished in the other more important skills. Your work on strengthening areas more critical to success will pay off more quickly.

That's about it. There will be a lot more to learn, but the good part is that you can learn on the job if you just master a few basics. Put the basics into practice, add the new things you have learned along the way that have been effective, and you will be amazed at the results. I have listed a few source materials in Appendices II and III that you might find helpful.

Remember to have fun. I have a story to tell you about that. One time when I was covering a large territory in the Midwest, based in Kansas City, my parents came to visit our family during the Christmas holidays. As I had already used up all my vacation that year, I still had to work a few days before the holiday, so my father agreed to accompany me on a sales trip to the Des Moines, Iowa area. We decided to drive up the evening before to spend some time together and catch a football game that night on TV, and I would make the sales calls the next day. On the drive up, I realized I had forgotten to pack a dress shirt, so we stopped at a mall in Des Moines to buy one. As it turned out, we ran into one of the key people I was going to be seeing the next day, and I introduced him to my father.

The next day, I made a few calls while my Dad stayed in the car, reading a newspaper. It was blowing and snowing big time. When I got to the office of the customer we had seen the night before, he asked about my dad. When he learned that my dad was in the car reading, he insisted on inviting him in. My dad ended up sitting around with their truck drivers having donuts, coffee, and, of course, all kinds of wonderful Christmas goodies to enjoy as well. Later, the customer invited us to lunch (which we had not planned), included my father, and we had a great time. We covered a little business and had an enjoyable lunch as well. After all, it was Christmas time. I can remember, while driving home, my dad, who had been a plant worker, machinist, and later department foreman in a manufacturing career, was sitting there silent for a long time. He finally looked over at me and said with something like awe in his voice, "They really pay you for this?"

He just couldn't believe it.

I have enjoyed the fun and challenges of selling my whole life. Learn to do it well, and it can be a rewarding career.

And they'll pay you for doing it!

★ ★ ★ ★ ★
POINTS

- ★ Find mentors or coaches, they can help
- ★ Think about and practice responses to situations that come up often
- ★ Ask management for help but have your ideas ready first
- ★ Read and study: additional in-depth information will help you improve your skills
- ★ Maintain at least the minimum required levels of proficiency in all areas
- ★ Emphasize your strengths first, work on weaknesses later
- ★ Have fun, and they'll pay you for doing it!

CHAPTER 20: NOTES FOR SALES MANAGERS
Develop a Sales Force of Winners!

What do you see as your major role and mission as a sales manager? I submit it is to help your people become the best salespeople they can be. I assume you were chosen for the position because of your strong selling skills, and your ability to communicate those skills to others.

Don't just sit back and observe and make decisions about your salespeople based solely on their results. You will be more successful if you take a very active role with your sales team by spending the necessary time with each of them to maximize their potential for growth and ultimate success.

How is that accomplished in practice? It means you will be meeting with them at various intervals discussing the potential for their important accounts and their plans going forward to realize that potential. You will help them set goals. These should be achievable goals with a little stretch built in. People don't grow unless they are reaching out of their comfort zone.

You will follow up at appropriate intervals to track their progress, to identify and, if needed, to assist with problems that stand in the way. This requires you to make enough sales calls with them to see how each one is doing so you can recognize their strengths and build on those, and to work together to develop plans to shore up the areas where improvement is needed.

In sales the 80/20 rule applies more often than not. For those not familiar with the 80/20 rule, here is what Wikipedia says about it: "The principle was suggested by management thinker Joseph M. Juran. It was named after the Italian economist Vilfredo Pareto, who observed that 80% of income in Italy was received by 20% of the Italian population. The assumption is that most of the results in any situation are determined by a small number of causes."

When applied to sales it means that 80% of your results typically come from about 20% of your salespeople. That doesn't mean that you eliminate the 80% who are less than stellar performers or are perhaps underperforming. It means figuring out how to help those people to develop to the stage where their performance, while perhaps not reaching that of the top 20%, will justify their continued employment as producers. Some will never make it.

During a fair and well-communicated trial period, performance deficiencies should be well documented, help should be offered, and attempts to grow should be encouraged. Ultimately, when you identify someone who just won't or can't make it, you will need to take appropriate action. One of the most difficult responsibilities for a sales manager is terminating poor performers. Facing the situation and doing what may be necessary can be quite uncomfortable, so many sales managers let those situations go on much longer than they should. Generally, problem situations don't get better with time and should be handled promptly.

When you are making calls with your salespeople, what should you be looking for? Here are some suggestions:

1. **Have they planned appropriately? Do they have all the information needed for the call and can they access it easily?**
2. **Do they present themselves in a pleasant, likable way? Do they approach the customers in a manner designed to cultivate stronger relationships?**
3. **Are their presentations skills up to par? Have they explained the benefits of your products or services in a clear and compelling manner?**
4. **Do they ask appropriate open-ended questions which will unearth the customer's needs, which often go unstated?**
5. **Do they know when to stop and leave before losing the customer through "overselling"?**

You will develop your own standards and requirements over time. If they are doing anything on the sales call that makes you question the action or feel uncomfortable, put those items on the table after the call.

1. **Do you observe that your salesperson performs the appropriate follow up actions after important calls?**
2. **When needed, are your salespeople coordinating properly with management and others in the company before and/or after the calls to accomplish their objectives?**

Don't just observe, get in the game. While I'm not a proponent of taking over a sales call if the salesperson runs into problems, occasionally a little personable interaction between you and the salesperson with the customer is appropriate, works very well, and can often make calls more lively and profitable. In this case, you're not just sitting there quietly like a judge, saying nothing. As a general practice, it's good to discuss ahead of time what your role may be. In problem calls your goal is not to take over, but to make mental notes of the difficulties and discuss them with the salesperson afterwards. Most people learn more by doing than watching. After all, your role is to teach them how to do better, not to generate feelings of inadequacy as they watch you do their job for them. The follow up discussions reviewing their sales call performance can help them improve.

You can perform another vital role: to help salespeople reach higher level customers than they may be able to access on their own. Many important people respond well to being visited by someone a little farther up the chain. Occasionally you might even see a top person in a situation without the sales person present. If this occurs, be sure this is a company/customer relationship building experience and not a "selling" experience. The salesperson should be the point man and the responsible party in dealing with the customer. You can pave the way occasionally, but be sure to get out of the way when it's time for your salespeople to represent your company in the selling process.

In earlier parts of the book I suggest that salespeople focus on improving on their strengths in the critical selling skills, because those are what produce results. As a sales manager I didn't worry about weak areas in peripheral skills unless they were not up to what I perceived as minimum standards. I felt there is always time later to work on those areas.

I am also a firm believer in what is commonly called performance management. That means that you look for things each salesperson is doing well, and sincerely complement those skills or actions. Many salespeople are doing a job that requires a high level of individual performance, often without close supervision. Most, in my experience, have a strong need for your appreciation when they do things well. Managing performance through this approach is critical to encouraging and replicating the desired behaviors. It may be that the most important thing you can do is to recognize and respond appropriately to those needs. Some books listed in Appendix II can help you with the details of doing this well.

You are also the conduit between management and the sales force. That means you sometimes have to deal with management decisions that you may not agree with, or you feel are not in the salespeople's best interests. Before implementing those kinds of actions, my advice is to bring your concerns to management and attempt to get everything worked out before going forward. Obviously management should, and will, have the final say, but you are the voice for your sales force, so you might occasionally have to be willing to buck the system if needed. You will gain respect from your salespeople if you rise to their needs and their defense. Also you are their cheerleader with management when they deserve it for a strong performance. They want to know you are putting them forward on those occasions.

When you are a mentor, coach, and advocate for your salespeople, and give them sincere compliments when appropriate, you will have gone a long way in deserving their loyalty and respect. You will achieve great personal satisfaction as your salespeople grow to become top notch, successful contributors to your company. Your own management will notice and appreciate you, and reward you for that effort!

★★★★★
POINTS

★ Your job is to help your salespeople achieve their top potential

★ Discuss each customer's potential with your salespeople and plan for achieving it.

★ Follow up to track progress

★ Spend enough time with them to determine strengths and development areas and how those will be approached.

★ Don't be afraid to part ways with chronic underperformers.

★ On sales calls, let the salesperson lead. At that point you are in a training role, not a sales role.

★ Sincere compliments for things done well are critical. Never forget that. They work much better than criticism in producing and replicating desired behaviors

★ In your role as a conduit to management, be an advocate for your salespeople

★ Enjoy the reward of personal satisfaction when they achieve and grow

APPENDIX I: TERRITORY ORGANIZATION
Detailed Examples for Setting Up Call Plans

Setting up calling plans can be somewhat complicated and time consuming, so I have included here a more detailed example of each. The Sector Call Plan may be difficult to fully understand, but if you will study it in the context of the explanation, I believe the mechanics will become clear. You can also download this appendix from our website to work on it or to view it on a larger screen: **www.5starselling.com**

SECTOR CALL PLAN METHOD

To illustrate this first approach, we will set up a plan based on mythical companies as if you are covering several states in the U.S. Any relation of the names of these companies to any real companies is purely coincidental. This same plan can be easily adapted if you are covering several countries, or only covering one large city. Illustrated here is a plan for six groups (C-1 through C-3, and P-1 though P-3).

If you are not familiar with the area you have been assigned, hopefully your company or the former salespeople who have called on the accounts in your territory will have an idea of their total potential for your products or services. If this information is not available, you can try trade association data, the internet, or perhaps something like the Thomas Register to evaluate the size of the companies and the markets in which they operate. If your company does not have much information, you may be operating on educated guesswork at this point, but as you begin calling and generating more information, you can go back and make adjustments to the plan that you have developed. At any rate, using the best information you can find, put together a list of your accounts and their estimated potential. Note that potential sales are not usually the same as their total purchases. Potential sales would be the sales you would expect to obtain if everything went perfectly (that sometimes happens!). That doesn't mean the potential will not be difficult to achieve, but it's your ultimate goal at each account. At this point do not worry about where they are located. It should look something like the following chart.

★
Chart 1

Customers and Prospects: Total Potential		
Customers & Prospects	**Location**	**Potential Sales ($)**
Magnus Engineering		3,000,000
Worth Chemicals		2,500,000
Rainbow Paints		2,300,000
Allied Components		1,750,000
Corfu Tech		1,500,000
Quickor		1,250,000
Mine Forever		1,250,000
Work Systems		1,000,000
Advertised Excellence		900,000
Foundry Systems		865,000
Quality Printing		800,000
Jack's Colors		775,000
Gator Valves		765,000
Y-Not Materials		750,000
Argus Structural Products		700,000
Cities Direct Products		675,000
AA Plastics		545,000
Advanced Materials		450,000
Doody Fences		425,000
Harris Materials		425,000
National Service company		425,000
Differential Systems		425,000
Blastor Cleaning Materials		400,000
K-A Manufacturing		315,000
Gebmans Basic Products		295,000
Dead Eye Castings		285,000
Valley Equipment		280,000
Modern Technology		280,000
Best Baby Foods		275,000
Tough Stuff Fasteners		275,000
NY Sports		260,000

Customers and Prospects: Total Potential		
Customers & Prospects	Location	Potential Sales ($)
Easter Chemicals		260,000
Good Products		255,000
Sterling Coatings		255,000
Warbucks		250,000
Chemical Sealants		250,000
Weller Hospitals		215,000
Kiwatic Copy Systems		215,000
Cistern Catchalls		215,000
Durable Paints		215,000
Astor Automotive		185,000
Triple A Loaders		175,000
Fortune Enterprises		175,000
First Call Manufacturing		175,000
Neverland Toys		150,000
Hickory Furniture		125,000
Major's Hogs		125,000
Bluepoint Printing		125,000
Processing Excellence		115,000
Busters Mechanicals		100,000
Leaf Pharmaceuticals		100,000
Platoon Products		100,000
Adhesive Products		100,000
Copy Products		95,000
Flick Bug Repellents		95,000
Wonder Manufacturing		75,000

Your territory will obviously have customers/prospects that have considerably more or less potential, and your large and small customers and prospects can be much larger or much smaller than this example. In this hypothetical case, you can see you have customers and prospects whose estimated potentials range from $75,000 to $3,000,000 (figured annually). Although you may separate them into as many groups as you like, for this example I have chosen to divide them into three groups, as follows:

★

Group 1
$1,000,000 – $3,000,000 in potential business

Group 2
$300,000 – $999,000 in potential business

Group 3
$75,000 – $299,000 in potential business

They will be given a (C) designation (for customer) if we have a substantial portion of their potential business, and a (P) designation (for prospect) if we don't. There will be some C-1s, C-2s, C-3s, and some P-1s, P-2s, and P-3s. You may decide you don't need to designate them as either customers or prospects, but I feel that differentiation is important because there will be a difference in the way they are treated. However, if you decide to eliminate the customer or prospect label, just designate them as 1, 2, or 3. If you have been given a new "uncharted" territory to build up from scratch, you will usually have many more prospects and few, if any, customers and will be revising your plan more often as you learn additional information about their potential. Again, for ranking purposes, the location of each account is not important.

Evaluating current sales to potential and assigning the accounts to these categories results in Chart 2.

★
CHART 2

Potential Sales and Actual Sales				
Customers and Prospects	Location	Potential Sales ($)	Actual Sales ($)	Rank
Magnus Engineering		3,000,000	2,000,000	C-1
Worth Chemicals		2,500,000	0	P-1
Rainbow Paints		2,300,000	100,000	P-1
Allied Components		1,750,000	765,000	C-1
Corfu Tech		1,500,000	750,000	C-1
Quickor		1,250,000	0	P-1
Mine Forever		1,250,000	150,000	P-1
Work Systems		1,000,000	400,000	C-1
Advertised Excellence		900,000	300,000	C-2
Foundry Systems		865,000	0	P-2
Quality Printing		800,000	100,000	P-2
Jack's Colors		775,000	335,000	C-2
Gator Valves		765,000	255,000	C-2
Y-Not Materials		750,000	0	P-2
Argus Structural Products		700,000	400,000	C-2
Cities Direct Products		675,000	300,000	C-2
AA Plastics		545,000	50,000	P-2
Advanced Materials		450,000	30,000	P-2
Harris Materials		425,000	10,000	P-2
Doody Fences		425,000	135,000	C-2
National Service company		425,000	150,000	C-2
Differential Systems		425,000	350,000	C-2
Blastor Cleaning Materials		400,000	25,000	P-2
K-A Manufacturing		315,000	0	P-2
Gebmans Basic Products		295,000	0	P-3
Dead Eye Castings		285,000	0	P-3
Modern Technology		280,000	0	P-3
Valley Equipment		280,000	100,000	C-3
Tough Stuff Fasteners		275,000	50,000	P-3
Best Baby Foods		275,000	125,000	C-3

Potential Sales and Actual Sales				
Customers and Prospects	Location	Potential Sales ($)	Actual Sales ($)	Rank
NY Sports		260,000	25,000	P-3
Easter Chemicals		260,000	35,000	P-3
Good Products		255,000	125,000	C-3
Sterling Coatings		255,000	125,000	C-3
Warbucks		250,000	150,000	C-3
Chemical Sealants		250,000	175,000	C-3
Cistern Catchalls		215,000	0	P-3
Kiwatic Copy Systems		215,000	10,000	P-3
Durable Paints		215,000	25,000	P-3
Weller Hospitals		215,000	110,000	C-3
Astor Automotive		185,000	55,000	C-3
Triple A Loaders		175,000	0	P-3
Fortune Enterprises		175,000	20,000	P-3
First Call Manufacturing		175,000	175,000	C-3
Neverland Toys		150,000	70,000	C-3
Hickory Furniture		125,000	0	P-3
Major's Hogs		125,000	5,000	P-3
Bluepoint Printing		125,000	10,000	P-3
Processing Excellence		115,000	0	P-3
Adhesive Products		100,000	0	P-3
Busters Mechanicals		100,000	65,000	C-3
Leaf Pharmaceuticals		100,000	65,000	C-3
Platoon Products		100,000	65,000	C-3
Flick Bug Repellents		95,000	60,000	C-3
Copy Products		95,000	80,000	C-3
Wonder Manufacturing		75,000	75,000	C-3

Next, to achieve efficiency, we will consider location. Look over the accounts and do your best to divide them into different geographic areas or sectors so you will be making the best use of your time when seeing them. For this plan, I will be using the term geographic area or sector interchangeably. You assign the accounts to different areas/sectors by observation or some method like putting pins or dots on a map. You don't need different colors depending on whether they are customers or prospects, but I suggest different colored pins or stickers for the 1s, 2s and 3s. As you do this, you may find your territory is small and you don't need sectors, or you may find you have several distinct areas to cover. It is best if you try to get by with as few sectors as possible, and then you will be able to see the customers and prospects more often (generally a good thing). For this method to work best, it is good to have about the same number of 1s and 2s in each sector or geographic area you will be covering. It doesn't matter if they are customers or prospects at this point, only that you have approximately the same number of high importance and medium importance accounts in each area. Don't worry about the smaller accounts (C-3s and P-3s), just add them to the appropriate geographic sectors or areas where they fit. Your first effort may look something like the next chart. For the example, we have assumed you have to cover four different areas and the following hypothetical companies within your territory as efficiently as possible. Again, although this chart covers specific cities, it could just as well apply to calls in different countries, states, or only one city.

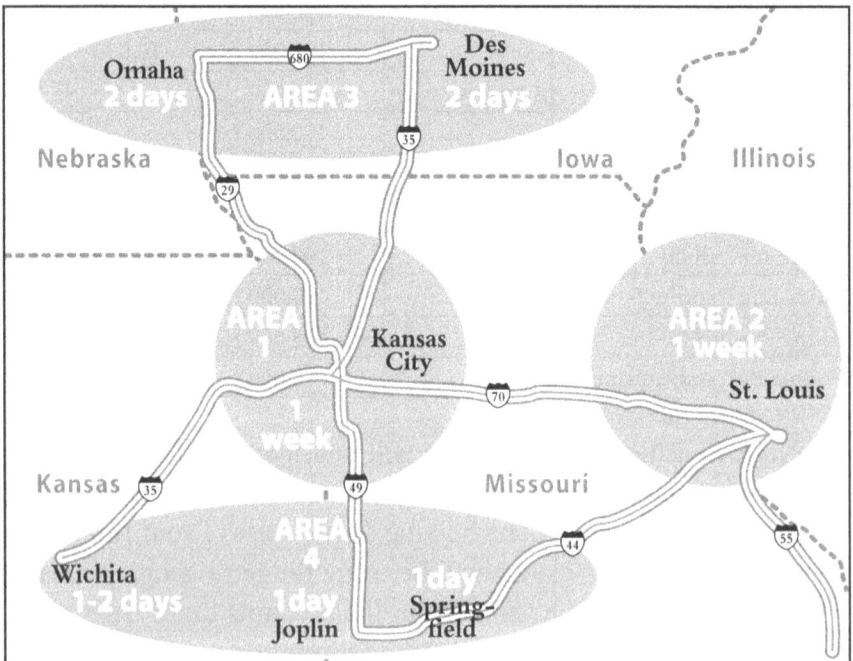

★
Chart 3

Potential Sales and Actual Sales				
Customers and Prospects	Location	Potential Sales ($)	Actual Sales ($)	Rank
Magnus Engineering	Area 1	3,000,000	2,000,000	C-1
Worth Chemicals	Area 1	2,500,000	0	P-1
Rainbow Paints	Area 3	2,300,000	100,000	P-1
Allied Components	Area 4	1,750,000	765,000	C-1
Corfu Tech	Area 2	1,500,000	750,000	C-1
Quickor	Area 4	1,250,000	0	P-1
Mine Forever	Area 2	1,250,000	150,000	P-1
Work Systems	Area 3	1,000,000	400,000	C-1
Advertised Excellence	Area 3	900,000	300,000	C-2
Foundry Systems	Area 3	865,000	0	P-2
Quality Printing	Area 1	800,000	100,000	P-2
Jack's Colors	Area 3	775,000	335,000	C-2
Gator Valves	Area 4	765,000	255,000	C-2
Y-Not Materials	Area 2	750,000	0	P-2
Argus Structural Products	Area 1	700,000	400,000	C-2
Cities Direct Products	Area 2	675,000	300,000	C-2
AA Plastics	Area 1	545,000	50,000	P-2
Advanced Materials	Area 3	450,000	30,000	P-2
Harris Materials	Area 4	425,000	10,000	P-2
Doody Fences	Area 4	425,000	135,000	C-2
National Service company	Area 2	425,000	150,000	C-2
Differential Systems	Area 1	425,000	350,000	C-2
Blastor Cleaning Materials	Area 2	400,000	25,000	P-2
K-A Manufacturing	Area 4	315,000	0	P-2
Gebmans Basic Products	Area 1	295,000	0	P-3
Dead Eye Castings	Area 4	285,000	0	P-3
Modern Technology	Area 2	280,000	0	P-3
Valley Equipment	Area 3	280,000	100,000	C-3
Tough Stuff Fasteners	Area 1	275,000	50,000	P-3
Best Baby Foods	Area 2	275,000	125,000	C-3
NY Sports	Area 3	260,000	25,000	P-3

Potential Sales and Actual Sales				
Customers and Prospects	Location	Potential Sales ($)	Actual Sales ($)	Rank
Easter Chemicals	Area 3	260,000	35,000	P-3
Good Products	Area 3	255,000	125,000	C-3
Sterling Coatings	Area 2	255,000	125,000	C-3
Warbucks	Area 1	250,000	150,000	C-3
Chemical Sealants	Area 1	250,000	175,000	C-3
Cistern Catchalls	Area 2	215,000	0	P-3
Kiwatic Copy Systems	Area 4	215,000	10,000	P-3
Durable Paints	Area 1	215,000	25,000	P-3
Weller Hospitals	Area 4	215,000	110,000	C-3
Astor Automotive	Area 4	185,000	55,000	C-3
Triple A Loaders	Area 4	175,000	0	P-3
Fortune Enterprises	Area 2	175,000	20,000	P-3
First Call Manufacturing	Area 1	175,000	175,000	C-3
Neverland Toys	Area 2	150,000	70,000	C-3
Hickory Furniture	Area 3	125,000	0	P-3
Major's Hogs	Area 4	125,000	5,000	P-3
Bluepoint Printing	Area 2	125,000	10,000	P-3
Processing Excellence	Area 3	115,000	0	P-3
Adhesive Products	Area 1	100,000	0	P-3
Busters Mechanicals	Area 3	100,000	65,000	C-3
Leaf Pharmaceuticals	Area 4	100,000	65,000	C-3
Platoon Products	Area 1	100,000	65,000	C-3
Flick Bug Repellents	Area 4	95,000	60,000	C-3
Copy Products	Area 3	95,000	80,000	C-3
Wonder Manufacturing	Area 2	75,000	75,000	C-3

Using the information in the previous chart, you can then prepare a simple sector or area call plan like the following. This example plan is based on four sectors, so visits to each sector would happen every month. The frequency of calling in each sector also depends on the time allotted to cover each sector. In our example we are assuming each sector requires a week to cover appropriately. However, as mentioned, there can be more or fewer sectors, depending on the geography.

★
CHART 4

Sector Call Plan				
Area	Customers & Prospects	Rank	Calls/ Year	Interval
1	Magnus Engineering	C-1	12	Every month
1	Worth Chemicals	P-1	12	Every month
1	Argus Structural Products	C-2	6	Every other month
1	Differential Systems	C-2	6	Every other month
1	Quality Printing	P-2	6	Every other month
1	AA Plastics	P-2	6	Every other month
1	Warbucks	C-3	4	Once a quarter
1	Chemical Sealants	C-3	4	Once a quarter
1	First Call Manufacturing	C-3	4	Once a quarter
1	Platoon Products	C-3	4	Once a quarter
1	Gebmans Basic Products	P-3	4	Once a quarter
1	Tough Stuff Fasteners	P-3	4	Once a quarter
1	Durable Paints	P-3	4	Once a quarter
1	Adhesive Products	P-3	4	Once a quarter
2	Corfu Tech	C-1	12	Every month
2	Mine Forever	P-1	12	Every month
2	Cities Direct Products	C-2	6	Every other month
2	National Service	C-2	6	Every other month
2	Y-Not Materials	P-2	6	Every other month
2	Blastor Cleaning	P-2	6	Every other month
2	Best Baby Foods	C-3	4	Once a quarter
2	Sterling Coatings	C-3	4	Once a quarter
2	Neverland Toys	C-3	4	Once a quarter
2	Wonder Manufacturing	C-3	4	Once a quarter
2	Modern Technology	P-3	4	Once a quarter
2	Cistern Catchalls	P-3	4	Once a quarter
2	Fortune Enterprises	P-3	4	Once a quarter
2	Bluepoint Printing	P-3	4	Once a quarter
3	Work Systems	C-1	12	Three times per quarter

Sector Call Plan				
Area	Customers & Prospects	Rank	Calls/ Year	Interval
3	Rainbow Paints	P-1	12	Three times per quarter
3	Advertised Excellence	C-2	6	Every other month
3	Jack's Colors	C-2	6	Every other month
3	Foundry Systems	P-2	6	Every other month
3	Advanced Materials	P-2	6	Every other month
3	Valley Equipment	C-3	4	Once a quarter
3	Good Products	C-3	4	Once a quarter
3	Busters Mechanicals	C-3	4	Once a quarter
3	Copy Products	C-3	4	Once a quarter
3	NY Sports	P-3	4	Once a quarter
3	Easter Chemicals	P-3	4	Once a quarter
3	Hickory Furniture	P-3	4	Once a quarter
3	Processing Excellence	P-3	4	Once a quarter
4	Allied Components	C-1	12	Every month
4	Quickor	P-1	12	Every month
4	Gator Valves	C-2	6	Every other month
4	Doody Fences	C-2	6	Every other month
4	Harris Materials	P-2	6	Every other month
4	K-A Manufacturing	P-2	6	Every other month
4	Weller Hospitals	C-3	4	Once a quarter
4	Astor Automotive	C-3	4	Once a quarter
4	Leaf Pharmaceuticals	C-3	4	Once a quarter
4	Flick Bug Repellents	C-3	4	Once a quarter
4	Dead Eye Castings	P-3	4	Once a quarter
4	Kiwatic Copy Systems	P-3	4	Once a quarter
4	Triple A Loaders	P-3	4	Once a quarter
4	Major's Hogs	P-3	4	Once a quarter

You may then prepare a worksheet for this four-sector approach and attach it to the plan. It should resemble the following example.

★
CHART 5

Area	Customers and Prospects	Rank	Calls Per Yr.	Weeks, First Quarter											
				1	2	3	4	5	6	7	8	9	10	11	12
1	Magnus Engineering	C-1	12												
1	Worth Chemicals	P-1	12												
1	Argus Structural Products	C-2	6												
1	Differential Systems	C-2	6												
1	Quality Printing	P-2	6												
1	AA Plastics	P-2	6												
1	Warbucks	C-3	4												
1	Chemical Sealants	C-3	4												
1	First Call Manufacturing	C-3	4												
1	Platoon Products	C-3	4												
1	Gebmans Basic Products	P-3	4												
1	Tough Stuff Fasteners	P-3	4												
1	Durable Paints	P-3	4												
1	Adhesive Products	P-3	4												
2	Corfu Tech	C-1	12												
2	Mine Forever	P-1	12												
2	Cities Direct Products	C-2	6												
2	National Service Company	C-2	6												
2	Y-Not Materials	P-2	6												
2	Blastor Cleaning Materials	P-2	6												
2	Best Baby Foods	C-3	4												
2	Sterling Coatings	C-3	4												
2	Neverland Toys	C-3	4												
2	Wonder Manufacturing	C-3	4												
2	Modern Technology	P-3	4												
2	Cistern Catchalls	P-3	4												
2	Fortune Enterprises	P-3	4												
2	Bluepoint Printing	P-3	4												
3	Work Systems	C-1	12												
3	Rainbow Paints	P-1	12												

| | | | | Weeks, First Quarter | | | | | | | | | | | |
Area	Customers and Prospects	Rank	Calls Per Yr.	1	2	3	4	5	6	7	8	9	10	11	12
3	Advertised Excellence	C-2	6												
3	Jack's Colors	C-2	6												
3	Foundry Systems	P-2	6												
3	Advanced Materials	P-2	6												
3	Valley Equipment	C-3	4												
3	Good Products	C-3	4												
3	Busters Mechanicals	C-3	4												
3	Copy Products	C-3	4												
3	NY Sports	P-3	4												
3	Easter Chemicals	P-3	4												
3	Hickory Furniture	P-3	4												
3	Processing Excellence	P-3	4												
4	Allied Components	C-1	12												
4	Quickor	P-1	12												
4	Gator Valves	C-2	6												
4	Doody Fences	C-2	6												
4	Harris Materials	P-2	6												
4	K-A Manufacturing	P-2	6												
4	Weller Hospitals	C-3	4												
4	Astor Automotive	C-3	4												
4	Leaf Pharmaceuticals	C-3	4												
4	Flick Bug Repellents	C-3	4												
4	Dead Eye Castings	P-3	4												
4	Kiwatic Copy Systems	P-3	4												
4	Triple A Loaders	P-3	4												
4	Major's Hogs	P-3	4												

You will attempt to call on the companies in each area the appropriate number of times when each area is visited. C-1s and P-1s will be called on every time you are in the area. C-2s and P-2s would be called on every other time, and the C-3s and P-3s only once a quarter. You can make a note of the calls on the worksheet when you make them, and it will be readily apparent when calls are needed in the future.

If it is easier for you to visualize the call plan, you might put to-gether a proposed call schedule that looks like the one below. You would work this in cycles like a calendar, starting with Area 1, and proceeding through each area before starting over again.

★
CHART 6

Cycle 1			
Area 1	**Area 2**	**Area 3**	**Area 4**
P-1 Magnus Engineering	C-1 Corfu Tech	P-1 Rainbow Paints	C-1 Allied Components
C-1 Worth Chemicals	P-1 Mine Forever	C-1 Work Systems	P-1 Quickor
P-2 Quality Printing	P-2 Y-Not Materials	P-2 Foundry Systems	C-2 Gator Valves
C-2 Differential Systems	C-2 National Service Co.	P-2 Advanced Materials	C-2 Doody Fences
P-3 Gebmans Basic	P-3 Modern Technology	C-3 Valley Equipment	P-3 Dead Eye Castings
C-3 Chemical Sealants	P-3 Fortune Enterprises	P-3 Hickory Furniture	P-3 Triple A Loaders

Cycle 2			
Area 1	**Area 2**	**Area 3**	**Area 4**
P-1 Magnus Engineering	C-1 Corfu Tech	P-1 Rainbow Paints	C-1 Allied Components
C-1 Worth Chemicals	P-1 Mine Forever	C-1 Work Systems	P-1 Quickor
C-2 Argus Structural.	C-2 Cities Direct	C-2 Jack's Colors	P-2 Harris Materials
P-2 AA Plastics	P-2 Blastor Cleaning	C-2 Ad Excellence	P-2 K-A Manufacturing
P-3 Tough Stuff Fastners	C-3 Best Baby Foods	P-3 NY Sports	P-3 Kiwatic Copy
C-3 First Call Mfg.	C-3 Neverland Toys	P-3 Proc. Excellence	P-3 Major's Hogs

Cycle 3			
Area 1	**Area 2**	**Area 3**	**Area 4**
P-1 Magnus Engineering	C-1 Corfu Tech	P-1 Rainbow Paints	C-1 Allied Components
C-1 Worth Chemicals	P-1 Mine Forever	C-1 Work Systems	P-1 Quickor
P-2 Quality Printing	P-2 Y-Not Materials	P-2 Foundry Systems	C-2 Gator Valves
C-2 Differential Systems	C-2 National Service Co.	P-2 Advanced Materials	C-2 Doody Fences
C-3 Warbucks	C-3 Sterling Coatings	P-3 Easter Chemicals	C-3 Weller Hospitals
P-3 Adhesive Products	P-3 Bluepoint Printing	C-3 Buster's Mechanical	C-3 Leaf Pharmaceuticals

Cycle 4			
Area 1	**Area 2**	**Area 3**	**Area 4**
P-1 Magnus Engineering	C-1 Corfu Tech	P-1 Rainbow Paints	C-1 Allied Components
C-1 Worth Chemicals	P-1 Mine Forever	C-1 Work Systems	P-1 Quickor
C-2 Argus Struct.ural	C-2 Cities Direct	C-2 Jack's Colors	P-2 Harris Materials
P-2 AA Plastics	P-2 Blastor Cleaning	C-2 Ad. Excellence	P-2 K-A Manufacturing
P-3 Durable Paints	P-3 Cistern Catchalls	C-3 Good Products	C-3 Astor Automotive
C-3 Platoon Products	C-3 Wonder Mfg	C-3 Copy Products	C-3 Flick Bug Repellents

You probably will not have the same number of calls in each area for each cycle as in the example, but this should give you the idea of how it works.

As noted above, you would work Cycle 1 all the way through, then Cycle 2 all the way through, etc., until you have worked Cycle 4 all the way through. Then start over. As you can see from the sector or area call plan we have put together, you are calling on your largest customers every time you make a cycle through each area. That may be every week, or every month; it just depends on how many areas/

sectors you have to cover and how long it takes to cover each sector or area. Of course, some customers may not want or need you to call as frequently as the plan suggests. Obviously you will want to accede to their wishes while at the same time making sure that when you do call, you are not wasting their time but have something new or important to offer. Sometimes an email or phone call — in between or as a replacement for a "normal" call on your plan — will fill the bill in those circumstances.

This kind of plan takes time to set up, but once you have it in place you can almost put your call frequency on autopilot and work on other important needs. It's also easy to adjust if changes are required.

Contact Call Plan Method

As mentioned in Chapter 2, the Contact Call Plan may be used effectively when you have to see many contacts at the same accounts. For example, this would be an excellent plan to use when dealing with large corporate accounts. Using a few of the accounts from our hypothetical territory, your plan should start out looking something like this (I have illustrated the plan for a 20-week period).

★
CHART 7

Customer Contact Call Plan

Customer	Calls/ Year	Week Number																			
		1	2	3	4	5	6	7	8	9	10	11	12	13	14	15	16	17	18	19	20
Magnus Engineering																						
Jim Baker (Purchasing)	26																					
Ed Snyder (Lab)	12																					
Doris Hall (Lab)	6																					
Florence Bell (Mfg)	2																					
Bill Wake (Mfg)	4																					
Bob Mann (Tech)	4																					
Sally Dunn (Orders)	6																					
Frank Stemm (Mkting)	3																					
Worth Chemicals																						
Dan Benson (Dir Purch)	12																					
Mary Quinn (Buyer)	26																					
Bill Burris (Lab)	6																					
Dave Springer (Mfg)	3																					
Mary Denton (Dir Mkting)	2																					
AA Plastics																						
John Marsh (Purchasing)	12																					
Kathy Davis (Buyer)	12																					
Bob Dark (Tech)	4																					
Aberdeen Furniture																						
Bill Plank (Buyer)	6																					

After you've been following it for awhile, and putting in the call information, it should look something like this:

★
CHART 8

Customer Contact Call Plan

Customer	Calls/Year	1	2	3	4	5	6	7	8	9	10	11	12	13	14	15	16	17	18	19	20
Magnus Engineering										V					V						
Jim Baker (Purchasing)	26		C		L		C		C	V	L		C		V	C	D		X		
Ed Snyder (Lab)	12		C						L	V			C		V						C
Doris Hall (Lab)	6								L	V					V	C					
Florence Bell (Mfg)	2					C				V					V						C
Bill Wake (Mfg)	4				C					V					V	C					
Bob Mann (Tech)	4					C				V					V		C				
Sally Dunn (Orders)	6		L					C		V					V		C				
Frank Stemm (Mkting)	3							C		V					V						
Worth Chemicals										V					V						
Dan Benson (Dir Purch)	12			E			X			V	L				V	X					L
Mary Quinn (Buyer)	26		C		C		C		C	V	C		C		V	L		C	C		
Bill Burris (Lab)	6			L						V	C				V						L
Dave Springer (Mfg)	3					C				V				G	V						
Mary Denton (Dir Mkting)	2			E						V					V						
AA Plastics										V					V						
John Marsh (Purchasing)	12				L				C	V			L		V	C					L
Kathy Davis (Buyer)	12				C				L	V			C		V						C
Bob Dark (Tech)	4				C					V					V	C					
Aberdeen Furniture										V					V						
Bill Plank (Buyer)	6		C							V			L		V						C

Symbols:
C= Call   L=Lunch   D=Dinner   G=Golf   V=Vacation
E= Major Entertainment (Theater, Fishing trip, etc.)

Of course, you can make up whatever symbols you want.

Either method will work very well. There are other approaches, but in my experience, one of these two types of call plans will fit most territories and accomplish the purpose of making the right number of calls on the right accounts (and contacts) at the right times. I used one or the other of these on several occasions with great success throughout my sales career. Put one of them together and stick with it. Organizing one of these plans takes care of the details and leaves you free to spend more time selling.

APPENDIX II: OTHER RESOURCES
Books

How to Win Friends and Influence People, by Dale Carnegie

See You at the Top, by Zig Ziglar

How I Raised Myself From Failure To Success In Selling, by Frank Bettger

How to Master the Art of Selling, by Tom Hopkins

Major Account Sales Strategy, by Neil Rackham and Richard Ruff

SPIN Selling and The SPIN Selling Fieldbook (a working follow-up tool for "Spin Selling"), by Neil Rackham

The New Strategic Selling, by Robert Miller, Stephen Heiman, and Tad Tuleja

The New Conceptual Selling, by Robert Miller, Stephen Heiman, and Tad Tuleja

The One Minute Salesperson, by Larry Wilson and Spencer Johnson

The Seven Habits of Highly Effective People, by Stephen Covey

Power Sales Writing: What Every Sales Person Needs to Know to Turn Prospects into Buyers, by Sue A. Hershkowitz

Bringing Out the Best in People: How to Apply the Astonishing Power of Positive Reinforcement, by Aubrey C. Daniels

Maximum Performance Management, by Joseph H. Boyett and Henry P. Conn

Secrets of Closing Sales, by Charles Roth and Roy Alexander

One on One: The Secrets of Professional Sales Closing, by R. Ian Seymour

Sales Closing for Dummies, by Tom Hopkins

The Secrets of Closing the Sale, by Zig Ziglar

The Art of Negotiating, by Gerard I. Nierenberg

Getting to Yes, Negotiating Agreement Without Giving In, by Roger Fisher and William Ury

The Lost Art of Listening, by Michael P. Nichols

Interactions 2: Listening/Speaking, by Judith Tanka and Lida R. Baker

The Business of Listening, by Diane Bonet

Appendix III:
Other Resources: Software

The business software market is very fluid and changes constantly. These are a few interesting starting points but many others are available. It may be worthwhile to employ your favorite search engine for alternate possibilities.

CRM(Customer Resource Management) Software

salesforce.com
netsuite.com
zoho.com
sugar.com
crmdynamics.com
na.sage.com
oncontact.com
infusionsoft.com

ERP (Enterprise Resource Planning) Software

plex.com
Sage ERP 100
Microsoft Dynamics

Lead Generation Software / Lead Management Software

leadmesh.com
leads360.com
dundas.com/dashboard

PROPHET CONTACT MANAGEMENT SOFTWARE

avidian.com

SAGE ACT! CONTACT AND CUSTOMER MANAGEMENT SOFTWARE

act.com

VIDEO TELEPHONE SOFTWARE

skype.com
google.com/talk

VIDEO CONFERENCING SOFTWARE

fuzebox.com
gotomeeting.com
nefsis.com
megameeting.com
trueconf.com

PRESENTATION SOFTWARE

Microsoft PowerPoint
prezi.com

ACKNOWLEDGMENTS

I am indebted to my son Ryan for the incentive to write this book. He was a typical kid who, from age 15 to about 25 thought he knew way more than his Dad about almost everything. However, when he decided to embark on a sales career with a company whose training program was sadly lacking, Dad suddenly became his go-to "Answer Man."

Since several excellent sales books had helped me with new ideas during my career, I searched for one or two that would take care of Ryan's needs as he began his new sales job. Unfortunately, it seemed most of the books were targeted at different, typically more complex sales issues, and were primarily oriented toward the seasoned salesperson. I finally decided that the timeless, critical, basic skills necessary to sell successfully that I had learned during my extensive sales career would be valuable to both Ryan and to many other new salespeople. As a result, this book was born.

Thanks also go to my wife Jacque, whose patience was impressive. I'm not sure she thought she'd ever see a finished product.

Also thanks to several people who were willing to read an early copy and offer useful comments for improvement. Those included David Reynolds, Greg Osterholt, Jim Cederna, Jay McQuillan, Jim Welch, Jim McGee, Stephanie Brady, Nigel Bell, Erin Davis, Ron Tepner, and Murray Deal. I want to give special thanks to Gare Calhoun for his hard work in the creation and maintenance of the book's website: **www.5starselling.com.** I also want to recognize the hard work of my editor, Mary de Wit, whose language skills and clear thinking helped me convey exactly what I intended to express.

Writing a book was an interesting and rewarding experience. I hope you benefit from reading it as much as I enjoyed writing it.

— *Lee Davis*

ABOUT THE AUTHOR
Lee Davis

For over 35 years, Lee Davis excelled in selling and sales management for a Fortune 500 company. In this concise and incisive book, he brings his experience and expertise to individuals who want to accelerate their sales careers. He consults in market research and offers sales training to companies who would benefit from his proven methods for success as their sole or supplemental sales program.

Lee Davis

Lee and his wife, Jacque, travel extensively, enjoy the scenic beauty of America, and visit the parks, monuments, and museums that exhibit our impressive national heritage.

If you would like to contact Lee with comments or suggestions, feel free to email him at **info@5starselling.com.**

www.ingramcontent.com/pod-product-compliance
Lightning Source LLC
Chambersburg PA
CBHW071234210326
41597CB00016B/2049